ZONDERVAN

Charts

CHRONOLOGICAL AND BACKGROUND

CHARTS OF THE

NEW
TESTAMENT

2ND EDITION

Books in the ZondervanCharts Series

Charts of Ancient and Medieval Church History *(John D. Hannah)*

Charts of Apologetics and Christian Evidences *(H. Wayne House and Joseph M. Holden)*

Charts of Bible Prophecy *(H. Wayne House and Randall Price)*

Charts of Christian Ethics *(Craig Vincent Mitchell)*

Charts of Christian Theology and Doctrine *(H. Wayne House)*

Charts of Cults, Sects, and Religious Movements *(H. Wayne House)*

Charts of Modern and Postmodern Church History *(John D. Hannah)*

Charts of Philosophy and Philosophers *(Craig Vincent Mitchell)*

Charts of Reformation and Enlightenment Church History *(John D. Hannah)*

Charts of the Gospels and the Life of Christ *(Robert L. Thomas)*

Charts of World Religions *(H. Wayne House)*

Chronological and Background Charts of Church History *(Robert C. Walton)*

Chronological and Background Charts of the New Testament *(H. Wayne House)*

Chronological and Background Charts of the Old Testament *(John H. Walton)*

Chronological and Thematic Charts of Philosophies and Philosophers *(Milton D. Hunnex)*

Taxonomic Charts of Theology and Biblical Studies *(M. James Sawyer)*

Timeline Charts of the Western Church *(Susan Lynn Peterson)*

ZONDERVAN

Charts

CHRONOLOGICAL AND BACKGROUND

CHARTS OF THE

NEW
TESTAMENT

2ND EDITION

H. Wayne House

RESEARCH ASSISTANCE — BART BOX

ZONDERVAN®

ZONDERVAN.com/
AUTHORTRACKER
follow your favorite authors

ZONDERVAN

Chronological and Background Charts of the New Testament, Second Edition
Copyright © 1981, 2009 by H. Wayne House

Requests for information should be addressed to:

Zondervan, Grand Rapids, Michigan 49530

Library of Congress Cataloging-in-Publication Data

House, H. Wayne.
    Chronological and background charts of the New Testament.
    Bibliography:
        p. cm.
    ISBN 978-0-310-28293-8
    1. Bible. N.T.—Handbooks, manuals, etc. I. Title. II. Series.
BS230.H68 2009
225.6'1 AACR2   81-130099

---

09 10 11 12 13 14 15 • 23 22 21 20 19 18 17 16 15 14 13 12 11 10 9 8 7 6 5 4 3 2 1

I desire to dedicate this book to three people:

Daniel Preston, my first-year Bible instructor at Tomlinson College, who inspired me toward serious Bible study;

Robert Gooch, a generous man of God who supported me through finances and prayer when I was in residence toward my doctorate;

Leta, my wife, who has been patient through many years of undergraduate and graduate work and the endless hours required to complete this book. She is my best critic and friend.

Contents

Foreword

When working with the New Testament, one soon realizes the enormous amount of data within it. Many times it is difficult to see how the various factors mentioned in the New Testament relate to each other. Or other interesting questions may be raised: How many miracles are there, and what Gospels record them? When was Paul at Corinth? What books did Paul write on his second missionary journey? Who were the leading statesmen and thinkers in the Roman Empire during Christ's ministry? One could go on.

Chronological and Background Charts of the New Testament will serve as a useful tool to Bible students in their search for answers to questions mentioned above, as well as to a myriad of other facts. Wayne House has put in one volume information that would take a library of books to give, in a format beneficial to all who read and study their Bible.

I hope many will utilize the materials in this book so that they will have a clear understanding of God's message revealed in the Holy Scriptures.

Harold W. Hoehner
Distinguished Professor of New Testament
Dallas Theological Seminary

Preface to the Second Edition

The first edition of *Chronological and Background Charts of the New Testament* was published more than a quarter-century ago. This was my very first book, one that continues to have value for students, pastors, and others in their study of the New Testament. This new edition updates some information and also corrects some minor errors, typos, and discrepancies.

I have also added a number of new charts that will prove helpful to the reader. These include various parallel and similarity charts, such as Luke and Acts, Matthew and Mark, Luke and Mark and Ephesians and Colossians, and 2 Peter and Jude. Some new charts deal with authorship—for example, Ephesians, Colossians, 2 Thessalonians, the Pastorals, and 2 Peter. Other new charts concern the date of Revelation and the Jesus Seminar's perspectives on the Gospels.

I have been encouraged over the years by comments from students, pastors, and professors who have found the New Testament charts book helpful to them in their academic training and useful as a reference after college and seminary. It is truly gratifying to produce a book that has been of such value to tens of thousands.

I need to give appreciation to those who have made suggestions over the years, particularly students of mine who have used the book. Also, much thanks is due to the Rev. Bart Box, who as a student at New Orleans Baptist Seminary provided some important research work on the charts book. His assistance was invaluable. I also wish to thank research assistant Robert Drouhard, who helped me on the project.

I would be remiss not to thank again Stanley Gundry in suggesting the revision and Jim Ruark for his excellent editing work. I must also give my appreciation to Dr. Harold Hoehner of Dallas Theological Seminary and Dr. Craig Blomberg of Denver Seminary for carefully reviewing the first edition, making numerous corrections and suggestions about how to make the second edition a much better work.

Last of all, I hope that this second edition will prove valuable to many more thousands of students of the New Testament, all to the glory of our God and Savior Jesus Christ.
Soli Deo Gloria!

H. Wayne House
Distinguished Research Professor,
Biblical and Theological Studies
Faith Evangelical Seminary
Tacoma, Washington
Columbus Day, October 13, 2008

Preface to the First Edition

In 1978 John H. Walton's *Chronological Charts of the Old Testament* was published and had an instant positive response from teachers and students of the Old Testament. This book filled a need for a reference tool on the myriad facts in the Old Testament and its historical background. Being a professor of New Testament, I sensed the need for a New Testament counterpart. Therefore I was delighted when Zondervan asked me to write such a book.

This reference tool to the New Testament and its times is intended for several audiences. Scholars may refer to it for examination of different points of view; for example, the duration of the ministry of Christ or the arguments on the authorship of Hebrews. The Bible student, pastor, or Bible teacher will find presentation of historical, cultural, chronological, and comparative information. The book covers issues of canon, gospel studies, textual criticism, biblical theology, ancient history, and numerous others.

I have sought to include the kind of information about which my students of New Testament have inquired or which I thought would be useful to the general Bible student. No attempt has been made to explain thoroughly all the topics presented. This book is intended to start a student on his way toward a comprehensive view of the subject in question. It should not be used as a substitute for in-depth study. Even though scholars disagree on dating, historical facts, meterology, chronology, and other matters, I have sought to be fair to all views and to be accurate.

Many people have contributed to this work. I want to give a special word of appreciation to my many professors of Bible and theology at Western Conservative Baptist Seminary and Concordia Seminary, St. Louis. An expression of love and gratitude I offer to Daniel Preston. He nurtured my interest in the Bible while he was my Bible professor at Tomlinson College. Dr. Harold Hoehner and Dr. Elliott Johnson of Dallas Theological Seminary were a real encouragement to me for the past two years. Merland Miller wrote a thesis, listed in my bibliography, from which I was able to gain considerable information. I wish to thank Merland and Western Conservative Baptist Seminary for permission to borrow occasionally from his thesis. Merland has become my friend through our interchange over this awesome task. Several students have lent a hand, either in proofreading, typing, or some other task: Joel Barker, Stephanie Derksen, Vanessa Brandimore, Lorin Flagg, Chris Lange, Mark Lee, Dave Luckert, Steve Robinett, and Libby Stephens. To them I express my appreciation. I had to spend many hours away from my children, Carrie and Nathan, to write this book. I appreciate their patience.

Soli Deo Gloria!

H. Wayne House
LeTourneau College
Longview, Texas

PART I
General Material

Books of the New Testament
(arranged according to time of writing)

Book	Author	Time of Writing[1]	Place of Writing	Addressees
Galatians	Paul	49, just after 1st missionary journey	Antioch in Syria (?)	Christians in Pisidian Antioch, Iconium, Lystra, Derbe, and southern Galatia
1 Thessalonians	Paul	50–51, during 2nd missionary journey	Corinth	Christians in Thessalonica
2 Thessalonians	Paul	50–51, during 2nd missionary journey	Corinth	Christians in Thessalonica
1 Corinthians	Paul	55–56, during 3rd missionary journey	Ephesus	Christians in Corinth
2 Corinthians	Paul	55–56, during 3rd missionary journey	Macedonia	Christians in Corinth
Romans	Paul	55–57, during 3rd missionary journey	Corinth	Christians in Rome
James	James, half brother of Jesus	40s–early 60s	Probably Jerusalem	Jewish Christians of the Dispersion
Mark	John Mark	late 50s or early 60s	Rome	Most likely Roman Christians (perhaps facing persecution)
Philemon	Paul	60–62	Rome	Philemon, his family, and the church in his house at Colosse
Colossians	Paul	60–62	Rome	Christians in Colosse
Ephesians	Paul	60–62	Rome	Christians in the region around Ephesus
Luke	Luke	57–62	Probably Caesarea or Rome	A Christian Roman official

Book	Author	Time of Writing[1]	Place of Writing	Addressees
Acts	Luke	60–62	Rome	Same as above
Philippians	Paul	61–62	Rome	Christians in Philippi
1 Timothy	Paul	62–68	Macedonia	Timothy in Ephesus
Titus	Paul	62–68	Nicopolis	Titus in Crete
2 Timothy	Paul	63–68	Rome	Timothy in Ephesus
1 Peter	Peter	early-to-mid 60s	Rome	Christians in Pontus, Galatia, Cappadocia, Asia, and Bithynia
2 Peter	Peter	mid-to-late 60s	Rome	Christians in Pontus, Galatia, Cappadocia, Asia, and Bithynia
Matthew	Matthew	40–60	Probably Antioch in Syria	Jews in Syria or Palestine
Hebrews	Unknown[2] (Apollos, Luke, Barnabas, Priscilla?)	60s	Unknown	Jewish Christians in Rome or Jerusalem
Jude	Jude, half brother of Jesus	50s to 70s	Unknown	Christians in general
John	John	late 80s or early 90s	Ephesus	Christians and/or non-Christians in the region around Ephesus
1 John	John	late 80s or early 90s	Ephesus	Christians in the region around Ephesus
2 John	John	late 80s or early 90s	Ephesus	A church near Ephesus
3 John	John	late 80s or early 90s	Ephesus	Gaius, a Christian in the region around Ephesus
Revelation	John	mid 90s	Patmos, off coast of Asia Minor	Seven churches in western Asia Minor

[1] All dates are A.D. Date of writing, place of writing, and addresses are disputed among scholars. For representative dates by conservative scholars, see Merrill C. Tenney, *New Testament Survey*, rev. ed., edited by Walter M. Dunnett (Grand Rapids: Eerdmans, 1985); Robert G. Gromacki, *New Testament Survey* (Grand Rapids: Baker, 1989); Donald Guthrie, *New Testament Introduction*, 4th rev. ed. (Downers Grove, Ill.: InterVarsity Press, 1990); Robert H. Gundry, *A Survey of the New Testament*, 4th ed. (Grand Rapids: Zondervan, 2003); D. A. Carson and Douglas J. Moo, *An Introduction to the New Testament*, 2nd ed. (Grand Rapids: Zondervan, 2006).

[2] See chart on authorship of Hebrews for details.

The base for this chart is from Robert H. Gundry, *A Survey of the New Testament*, 4th ed. (Grand Rapids: Zondervan, 2003). Adapted by permission.

Books of the New Testament

English	Latin	Greek (with Translation)
Matthew	*Incipit Evangelium Secundum Matthaeus*	*Kata Maththaion*, According to Matthew
Mark	*Incipit Evangelium Secundum Marcus*	*Kata Markon*, According to Mark
Luke	*Incipit Evangelium Secundum Lucas*	*Kata Loukan*, According to Luke
John	*Incipit Evangelium Secundum Iohannes*	*Kata Iōannēn*, According to John
Acts	*Actus Apostolorum*	*Praxeis Apostolon*, Acts or Deeds of Apostles
Romans	*ad Romanos*	*Pro Rōmaious*, To the Romans
1 Corinthians	*ad Corinthios I*	*Korinthious a*, First (letter) to the Corinthians
2 Corintians	*ad Corinthios II*	*Korinthious b*, Second (letter) to the Corinthians
Galatians	*ad Galatas*	*Galatas*, To the Galatians
Ephesians	*ad Ephesios*	*Ephesious*, To the Ephesians
Philippians	*ad Philippenses*	*Philippēsious*, To the Philippians
Colossians	*ad Colossenses*	*Kolossaeis*, To the Colossians
1 Thessalonians	*ad Thessalonicenses I*	*Thessalonikeis a*, First (letter) to the Thessalonians
2 Thessalonians	*ad Thessalonicenses II*	*Thessalonikeis b*, Second (letter) to the Thessalonians
1 Timothy	*ad Timotheum I*	*Timotheon a*, First (letter) to Timothy
2 Timothy	*ad Timotheum II*	*Timotheon b*, Second (letter) to Timothy
Titus	*ad Titum*	*Titon*, To Titus
Philemon	*ad Philemonem*	*Philēmona*, To Philemon
Hebrews	*ad Hebraeos*	*Pros Hebraious*, To Hebrews
James	*Iacobi*	*Iakōbou*, Of James
1 Peter	*Petri I*	*Petrou a*, First (letter) of Peter
2 Peter	*Petri II*	*Petrou b*, Second (letter) of Peter
1 John	*Ioannis I*	*Iōannou a*, First (letter) of John
2 John	*Ioannis II*	*Iōannou b*, Second (letter) of John
3 John	*Ioannis III*	*Iōannou g*, Third (letter) of John
Jude	*Iudae*	*Iouda*, Jude
Revelation	*Apocalypsis*	*Apokalypsis Iōannou*, Revelation of John

Literary Classification of the New Testament

Biography[1]	History[2]	Pauline Epistles	General Epistles	Prophecy-Apocalypse[3]
Matthew Mark Luke John	Acts	Romans 1 Corinthians 2 Corinthians Galatians Ephesians Philippians Colossians 1 Thessalonians 2 Thessalonians 1 Timothy 2 Timothy Titus Philemon	Hebrews James 1 Peter 2 Peter 1 John 2 John 3 John Jude	Revelation

[1] These are not ordinary biographies but rather the unique stories of the life of Jesus Christ.

[2] Acts is not merely history in the sense of a record of historical data. It is interpretive theological history—Salvation history.

[3] The Book of Revelation shares similarities with Jewish apocalyptic works and later Old Testament books of apocalypticism, but also with Old Testament prophecy. Internally, the book is called a book of prophecy and an apocalypsis. Epistolary forms are also evident (e.g., Rev. 2–3).

Books of the New Testament Classified Doctrinally

Book	Classification	Theme
Matthew	Gospel—Good News of Jesus Christ	Jesus the Messiah as King
Mark	Gospel—Good News of Jesus Christ	Jesus the Messiah as Servant of Yahweh
Luke	Gospel—Good News of Jesus Christ	Jesus the Messiah as True Man
John	Gospel—Good News of Jesus Christ	Jesus the Messiah as Son of God
Acts	Theological history	Acts of the Holy Spirit through the church
Romans	Soteriology	Paul's interpretation of the gospel
1 Corinthians	Ecclesiology	Church problems
2 Corinthians	Ecclesiology	Ministry of Paul vindicated
Galatians	Soteriology	Liberation by the gospel
Ephesians	Christology	Christ as Lord over the church
Philippians	Christology	Joy in Christ
Colossians	Christology	Christ as Lord over the cosmos
1 Thessalonians	Eschatology	Second coming of Christ described
2 Thessalonians	Eschatology	Second coming of Christ clarified
1 Timothy	Ecclesiology	Pastoral care of a church
2 Timothy	Ecclesiology	Ministry of Paul completed and his final charge to his spiritual son
Titus	Ecclesiology	The proper traits of a church—sound doctrine and good works
Philemon	Personal note	Forgiveness and brotherhood in Christ
Hebrews	Christology-soteriology	Superiority of the priesthood of Christ and His salvation
James	Soteriology	Practical outworking of salvation
1 Peter	Eschatology	Christian response to suffering in anticipation of Christ's coming
2 Peter	Eschatology	Certainty of the gospel and the Day of the Lord
1 John	Soteriology	Assurance of personal salvation
2 John	Soteriology	Warning about false teaching
3 John	Personal note	Exhortation in view of domineering and malicious leader
Jude	Eschatology	Contending for the faith in view of Christ's coming
Revelation	Eschatology	Victory of Christ and the church over sin and the world

The base of this chart is from Irving Jensen, *1 Corinthians* (Chicago: Moody, 1972). Adapted by permission.

Theological Emphases and Order of New Testament Letters

Literary Classifi-cation	New Testament Book	Theological Category	Theological Emphasis
Gospels	Matthew		Jesus as King
	Mark		Jesus as Servant
	Luke		Jesus as Son of Man
	John		Jesus as Son of God
History	Acts		Birth and building of the church
Epistles, Pauline	Romans	Salvation	Explanation of the doctrine of salvation
	1 Corinthians	Church	Discussion of various aspects of Christian conduct
	2 Corinthians		Portrayal of the Christian ministry
	Galatians	Salvation	Implications of justification by faith
	Ephesians	Church as the body of Christ	Believer's position "in Christ"
	Philippians		Believer's attitude in Christ
	Colossians		Believer's completeness in Christ
	1 Thess.	Second Coming	Second Coming described
	2 Thess.		Second Coming clarified
	1 Timothy	Church organization	Conduct in house of God elucidated
	2 Timothy		Final charge to servant of God given
	Titus		Need for sound doctrine and good works stated
	Philemon	Personal note	Favor requested for a Christian brother
Epistles, General	Hebrews	Comfort and exhortation	Superiority of Christ and Christian life
	James		Need for good works as evidence of genuine faith
	1 Peter		Conduct and joy of believers in suffering
	2 Peter	Warning concerning false teaching	Gospel's certainty and the Day of the Lord
	1, 2, 3 John		Way of fellowship and genuine faith
	Jude		Warning concerning false teachers
Prophecy-Apocalypse	Revelation		Capstone of God's kingdom and redemptive programs

The base for this chart is from Stanley A. Ellisen, *Bible Workbook, Part VI: The Synoptic Gospels* (Portland, Ore.: Western Conservative Baptist Seminary, 1969; Stanley A. Ellisen, *The Book of Romans: God's Philosophy of Salvation*, Progressive Bible Studies (Portland, Ore.: Western Conservative Baptist Seminary, 1971). Adapted by permission.

The New Testament Canon in the First Four Centuries

Legend:
- X = Citation or allusion
- O = Named as authentic
- ? = Named as disputed

Book	Pseudo-Barnabas (c. 70–130)	Clement of Rome (c. 95–97)	Ignatius (c. 110)	Polycarp (c. 110–50)	Hermas (c. 115–40)	Didache (c. 120–50)	Papias (c. 130–40)	Irenaeus (c. 130–202)	Diognetus (c. 150)	Justin Martyr (c. 150–55)	Clement of Alexandria (c. 150–215)	Tertullian (c. 150–220)	Origen (c. 185–254)	Cyril of Jerusalem (c. 315–86)	Eusebius (c. 325–40)	Jerome (c. 340–420)	Augustine (c. 400)	Marcion (c. 140)	Muratorian (c. 170)	Barococcio (c. 206)	Apostolic (c. 300)	Cheltenham (c. 360)	Athanasius (367)	Tatian Diatessaron (c. 170)	Old Latin (c. 150–70)	Old Syriac (c. 200)	Nicea (c. 325–40)	Hippo (393)	Carthage (397)	Carthage (419)
Matt.	X	X	X	X	X	X	O	X	X	X	X	X	O	O	O	O	O		O	O	O	O	O	O	O	O	O	O	O	O
Mark	X	X	X	X	X	X	O	X	X	X	X	X	O	O	O	O	O		O	O	O	O	O	O	O	O	O	O	O	O
Luke	X	X	X	X	X	X	O	X	O	X	X	X	O	O	O	O	O	X	O	O	O	O	O	O	O	O	O	O	O	O
John	X	X	X	X	X	X	O	X	O	X	X	X	O	O	O	O	O		O	O	O	O	O	O	O	O	O	O	O	O
Acts		X	X		X		O	X		X	X	X	O	O	O	O	O		O	O	O	O	O		O	O	O	O	O	O
Rom.	X	X	X	X	X		O	X	X	X	X	X	O	O	O	O	O	O	O	O	O	O	O		O	O	O	O	O	O
1 Cor.	X	X	X	X	X		O	X	X	O	X	X	O	O	O	O	O	O	O	O	O	O	O		O	O	O	O	O	O
2 Cor.		X	X	X			O	X		O	X	X	O	O	O	O	O	O	O	O	O	O	O		O	O	O	O	O	O
Gal.	X	X	X	X			O	X		X	X	X	O	O	O	O	O	O	O	O	O	O	O		O	O	O	O	O	O
Eph.	X	X	X	X			O	X	X	X	X	X	O	O	O	O	O	O	O	O	O	O	O		O	O	O	O	O	O
Phil.	X	X	X	X			O	X		X	X	X	O	O	O	O	O	O	O	O	O	O	O		O	O	O	O	O	O
Col.			X	X			O	X	X		X	X	O	O	O	O	O	O	O	O	O	O	O		O	O	O	O	O	O
1 Thess.		X	X	X	X		O	X		X	X	X	O	O	O	O	O	O	O	O	O	O	O		O	O	O	O	O	O
2 Thess.		X	X	X	X		O	X		X	X	X	O	O	O	O	O	O	O	O	O	O	O		O	O	O	O	O	O
1 Tim.	X		X	X	X		X	X	X	O	X	X	O	O	O	O	O		O	O	O	O	O		O	O	O	O	O	O
2 Tim.	X		X	X			X	X	X		X	X	O	O	O	O	O		O	O	O	O	O		O	O	O	O	O	O
Titus	X	X		X			X	X	X	O	X	X	O	O	O	O	O		O	O	O	O	O		O	O	O	O	O	O
Philem.	X	X					X	X			O	X	O	O	O	O	O		O	O	O	O	O		O	O	O	O	O	O
Heb.	X	X		X	X		X		X	O	O	?	O	O	O	O	O			O	O		O		O	O	?	O	O	O
James	X	X	X	X	X		X		X	O	O	?	O	O	?	O	O			O	O	O	O		O	O	?	O	O	O
1 Peter	X	X	X	X			O	O	X	O	O	O	O	O	O	O	O			O	O	O	O		O	O	O	O	O	O
2 Peter	X	X		X			O	?		X	O	?	O	O	?	O	O			?	?	O	O		O		?	O	O	O
1 John		X		X			O	O	X	O	O	O	O	?	O	O	O		O	O	?	O	O		O	O	?	O	O	O
2 John		X					X	O			X	?	O	?	O	O	O		O	O	?	O	O		O		?	O	O	O
3 John												?	O	?	O	O	O			O	?	O	O		O		?	O	O	O
Jude	X	X	X		X	O	X	O	X	O	O	O	O	?	O	O	O		O	O	?	O	O		O		?	O	O	O
Rev.		X		X	X		O	O	X	O	O	O	O	?	?	O	O		O	O	O		O		O		?	O	O	O

Taken with adaptation from William E. Nix and Norman L. Geisler, *Introduction to the Bible* (Chicago: Moody, 1968). Used by permission. See also Bruce M. Metzger, *The Canon of the New Testament: Its Origin, Development and Significance* (New York: Oxford University Press, c. 1987, 1997).

Early Patristic Quotations of the New Testament

Writer	Gospels	Acts	Pauline Epistles	General Epistles	Revelation	Totals
Justin Martyr	268	10	43	6	3	330
Irenaeus	1,038	194	499	23	65	1,819
Clement of Alexandria	1,017	44	1,127	207	11	2,406
Origen	9,231	349	7,778	399	165	17,922
Tertullian	3,822	502	2,609	120	205	7,258
Hippolytus	734	42	387	27	188	1,378
Eusebius	3,258	211	1,592	88	27	5,176
Grand Totals	19,368	1,352	14,035	870	664	36,289

Note: Justin Martyr also made 266 allusions to various New Testament writings.

Taken with adaptation from William E. Nix and Norman L. Geisler, *Introduction to the Bible* (Chicago: Moody, 1968). Used by permission.

Theories concerning the History of the Text

I. Westcott and Hort

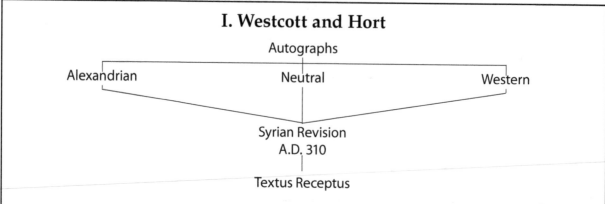

The Neutral group is highly favored as the correct reading. The antiquity of the MS evidence is the predominant external factor. The Majority (Byzantine) text-type is the result of a revision in A.D. 310 and is basically trustworthy.

II. Tischendorf

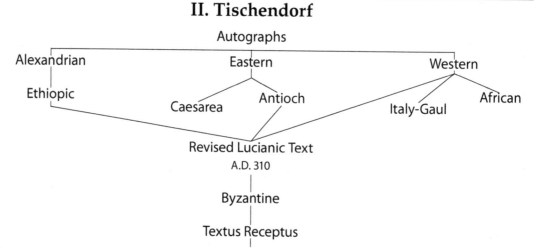

Consideration is given to both the ages of MSS and the geographical distribution of the MSS. The Byzantine MSS are believed to contain the better readings, at times, even over the older MSS.

III. Nestle-Aland

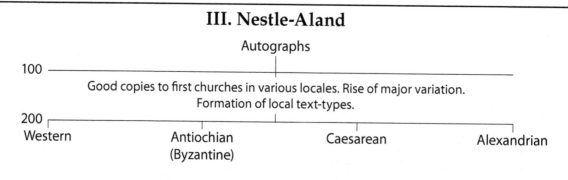

Each text-type, where it is attested by a concensus of its leading witnesses, is individually preserved from the end of the second century (A.D. 200). There was no fourth-century recension.

Liquid and Dry Measures

Measure	System Equivalent	Metric	U.S. Equivalent	KJV	NIV	NASB	Scripture Example
XESTÉS (Probably a corruption of Latin *sextarius*)	1/16 of a *modius*			pots	pitchers	pitchers	Mark 7:4
Dry		c. .47 lit	c. 1 pt				
Liquid		c. .47 lit	c. 1 pt				
CHOINIX							
Dry	2 *sextarii*	c. .95 lit	c. 1 qt	measure	quart	quart	Rev. 6:6
MODIOS (Latin *modius*)	16 *sextarii* 8 *choinikes*	c. 8.8 lit	c. ¼ bu	bushel	bowl	peck-measure	Matt. 5:15
Dry			c. 1 pk				
SATON (Hebrew *seah*)							
Dry	1½ *modi* according to Josephus	c. 11.4 lit	c. 12 qts c. 1.3 pks	measures	large amount	pecks	Matt. 13:33
BATOS (Hebrew *bath*)							
Liquid	72 *sextarii* 4½ *modii* according to Josephus	c. 34.2 lit	c. 7.6 gal c. 10½ gal	measures	gallons	measures	Luke 16:6
METRÉTÉS							
Liquid	c. equal to *batos* or Hebrew *bath*	c. 34.2 lit	c. 7.6 gal	firkins	gallons	gallons	John 2:6
KOROS (Hebrew *kor*, also known as *homer*)				measures	bushels	measures	Luke 16:7
Dry	c. 10 *metretai*	c. 396 lit	11.2 bu				
Liquid	c. 10 *metretai*	352–422 lit	10–11.98 gal				

Weights[1]

Measure	System Equivalent	Metric	U.S. Equivalent	KJV	NIV	NASB	Scripture Example
litra (Roman *libra*, 1 lb = 12 oz troy)		c. .340kg	c. 12 oz	pound	pounds	pounds	John 19:39
talanton[2]	c. 125 Roman *librae*	c. 34kg	c. 75 lbs	talent	100 pounds	100 pounds	Rev. 16:21

[1] Weights are avoirdupois rather than troy.
[2] Words referring to sums of money were also used in referring to weight.

Length and Distance

Measure	System Equivalent	Metric	U.S. Equivalent	KJV	NIV	NASB	Scripture Example
PĒCHYS	(forearm)	c. .45m	18 in (Hellenistic measurement) 21.6 in (Jewish)	200 cubits one cubit cubits	100 yards single hour cubits	100 yards cubit yards	John 21:8 Matt. 6:27 Rev. 21:17
ORGYIA	4 *pēchys* (arms outstretched horizontally)	c. 1.8m	c. 6 ft	20 fathoms	120 ft	20 fathoms	Acts 27:28
STADION	100 *orgyiai* (length of ancient Greek race course)	c. 177.6m	c. 575.75 ft	midst of the sea three score furlongs race 12,000 furlongs	considerable distance 7 miles race 12,000 stadia	many stadia 7 miles race 1,500 miles	Matt. 14:24 Luke 24:13 1 Cor. 9:24 Rev. 21:16
MILION	8 *stadia*, Roman mile (Roman *mille passuum*, "thousand paces"–5 Roman fit to the pace) Jewish = ½ of parasang, Persian measure or 7½ *stadia*	c. 1,500m 1.38km	c. 4,800 ft 4,500 ft	mile	mile	mile	Matt. 5:41
KALAMOS	measuring rod 6 long cubits	c. 3m	c. 10 ft	rod reed	measuring rod measuring rod	measuring rod measuring rod	Rev. 11:1 Rev. 21:15
Sabbath day's journey (based on rabbinical exegesis of Ex. 16:29 and Josh. 3:4)	c. 2,000 cubits (Josephus said it was 6 *stadia*) (little over half a mile)	c. 900m	c. 3,000 ft	sabbath day's journey	sabbath day's journey	sabbath day's journey	Acts 1:12

Money

Coinage	System Equivalent	U.S. Equivalent[1]	KJV	NIV	NASB	Scripture Example
Greek: drachma (*drachmē*)	day's wage	$52.40	pieces of silver	silver coins	silver coins	Luke 15:8
two drachmas (*didrachmon*)	2 days' wage	$104.80	tribute	two drachmas	two drachmas	Matt. 17:24
four drachmas (*statēr*)	4 days' wage	$209.60	piece of money	four drachmas	stater	Matt. 17:27
Roman: denarius (*dēnarion*)	day's wage	$52.40	pence penny	denarius silver coins day's wage	denarii denarii denarius	Matt. 18:28 Luke 10:35 Rev. 6:6
assarion	1/16 of a denarius or of a drachma	c. $3.28	farthing	penny	cent	Matt. 10:29
kodrantes	1/64 of a denarius or of a drachma	c. $.82	farthing	penny	cent	Matt. 5:26
lepton (Jewish ?)	1/128 of a denarius or of a drachma	$.21	mite	very small copper coins	small copper coins	Mark 12:42
argyrion (silver)	day's wage shekel, 4 drachmas or Attic silver, 1 drachma	$52.40	pieces of silver	penny silver coins drachma	cent pieces of silver pieces of silver	Luke 12:59 Matt. 26:15 Acts 19:19
chrysos (gold)	aureus (Roman coin) 25 denarii	$1,310.00	gold	gold	gold	Matt. 10:9
talanton	240 aurei (value of one silver talent)	$314,000.00[2]	talents	talents	talents	Matt. 18:24
mina (*mna*)	1/60 of a talent	$5,240.00[2]	pounds	minas	minas	Luke 19:13–25

[1]There is no exact formula for finding modern equivalents to ancient monetary units. Since the drachma—the basic monetary unit used in the ancient biblical world—was roughly one day's wages for a manual laborer, the equivalent one day's minimum wage is used here ($6.55 per hour as of 2008). To find what one drachma would be worth today, simply multiply the current minimum wage by 8 hours.

[2] Talent and mina also refer to weight. When monetary amount is intended, the value depends on whether the coins are silver or gold. *Chrysos* is the Greek word for gold, not for a specific coin; but in Matthew 10:9 it probably refers to money, either to the Roman *aureus* mentioned above, or to the half *aureus*, which Rome also circulated.

New Testament Quotations of Old Testament Passages

OT Passages	Gospels	Acts	Pauline Letters	General Letters
Gen.				
2:2				Heb. 4:4
2:7			1 Cor. 15:45	
2:24	Matt. 19:5; Mark 10:7–8		1 Cor. 6:16; Eph. 5:31	
12:1		7:3		
12:3		3:25	Gal. 3:8	
13:15			Gal. 3:16	
15:5			Rom. 4:18	
15:6			Rom. 4:3, 9, 22; Gal. 3:6	James 2:23a
15:13–14		7:6–7		
17:5			Rom. 4:17	
18:10			Rom. 9:9	
18:14			Rom. 9:9	
18:18		3:25	Gal. 3:8	
21:10			Gal. 4:30	
21:12			Rom. 9:7	
22:17				Heb. 11:18
22:18		3:25		Heb. 6:14
25:23			Rom. 9:12	
26:4		3:25		
Exod.				
2:14		7:27–28		
3:5		7:33–34		
3:6	Matt. 22:32; Mark 12:26; Luke 20:37	7:32		
3:7–10		7:33–34		
3:12		7:7b(?)		
9:16			Rom. 9:17	
12:46(?)	John 19:36			
13:2(?)	Luke 2:23			
13:12	Luke 2:23			
16:18			2 Cor. 8:15	
19:13				Heb. 12:20
20:12	Matt. 15:4; Mark 7:10		Eph. 6:2–3	
20:12–16	Matt. 19:18–19; Mark 10:19; Luke 18:20			
20:13	Matt. 5:21			James 2:11b
20:13–17			Rom. 13:9	
20:14	Matt. 5:27			James 2:11a
20:17			Rom. 7:7	
21:17	Matt. 15:4; Mark 7:10			
21:24	Matt. 5:38			
22:28		23:5		
24:8				Heb. 9:20
25:40				Heb. 8:5
32:6			1 Cor. 10:7	
33:19			Rom. 9:15	

OT Passages	Gospels	Acts	Pauline Letters	General Letters
Lev.				
11:44				1 Peter 1:16
12:8	Luke 2:24			
18:5			Rom. 10:5; Gal. 3:12	
19:2				1 Peter 1:16
19:18	Matt. 5:43; 19:19; 22:39; Mark 12:31; Luke 10:27		Rom. 13:9; Gal. 5:14	James 2:8
20:7				1 Peter 1:16
24:20	Matt. 5:38			
26:11–12			2 Cor. 6:16–18	
Num.				
9:12(?)	John 19:36			
16:5			2 Tim. 2:19	
Deut.				
5:16	Matt. 15:4; Mark 7:10			
5:16–20	Matt. 19:18–19; Mark 10:19; Luke 18:20		Eph. 6:2–3	
5:17	Matt. 5:21			James 2:11b
5:17–21			Rom. 13:9	
5:18	Matt. 5:27			James 2:11a
5:21			Rom. 7:7	
6:4–5	Matt. 22:37; Mark 12:29–30; Luke 10:27			
6:13	Matt. 4:10; Luke 4:8			
6:16	Matt. 4:7; Luke 4:12			
8:3	Matt. 4:4; Luke 4:4			
9:19				Heb. 12:21
18:15		3:22–23; 7:37		
18:18–19		3:22–23		
19:15	Matt. 18:16		2 Cor. 13:1	
21:23			Gal. 3:13	
24:1	Matt. 5:31			
25:4			1 Cor. 9:9; 1 Tim. 5:18	
27:26			Gal. 3:10	
29:4			Rom. 11:8	
30:12–14			Rom. 10:6–8	
31:6				Heb. 13:5
31:8				Heb. 13:5
32:21			Rom. 10:19	
32:35			Rom. 12:19–20	Heb. 10:30a
32:36				Heb. 10:30b
32:43			Rom. 15:10	
32:43 LXX				Heb. 1:6
Judges				
13:5–7(?)	Matt. 2:23			
1 Sam.				
7:14(?)			2 Cor. 6:16–18	Heb. 1:5b
1 Kings				
19:10, 14			Rom. 11:3	
19:18			Rom. 11:4	

OT Passages	Gospels	Acts	Pauline Letters	General Letters
Job				
5:13			1 Cor. 3:19	
41:11			Rom. 11:34–35	
Ps.				
2:1–2		4:25–26		
2:7		13:33		Heb. 1:5a; 5:5
5:9			Rom. 3:13	
8:3 LXX	Matt. 21:16			
8:4–6				Heb. 2:6–8
8:6			1 Cor. 15:27; Eph. 1:22	
14:1–3			Rom. 3:10–12	
16:8–11		2:25–28, 31		
16:10		13:35		
18:49			Rom. 15:9	
19:4			Rom. 10:18	
22:1	Matt. 27:46; Mark 15:34			
22:18	Matt. 27:35; John 19:24			
22:22				Heb. 2:12
24:1			1 Cor. 10:26	
31:5	Luke 23:46			
32:1–2			Rom. 4:7–8	
34:12–16				1 Peter 3:10–12
34:20(?)	John 19:36			
35:19	John 15:25			
36:1			Rom. 3:18	
40:6–8				Heb. 10:5–7
41:9	John 13:18			
44:22			Rom. 8:36	
45:6–7				Heb. 1:8–9
51:4			Rom. 3:4	
68:18			Eph. 4:8	
69:9	John 2:17		Rom. 15:3	
69:22–23			Rom. 11:9–10	
69:25		1:20		
78:2	Matt. 13:35			
82:6	John 10:34			
94:11			1 Cor. 3:20	
95:7–8				Heb. 3:15; 4:7
95:7–11				Heb. 3:7–11
95:11				Heb. 4:3, 5
102:25–27				Heb. 1:10–12
104:4				Heb. 1:7
109:8		1:20		
110:1	Matt. 22:44; Mark 12:36; Luke 20:42–43	2:34–35		Heb. 1:13
110:4				Heb. 5:6; 7:17, 21
112:9			2 Cor. 9:9	
116:10			2 Cor. 4:13	
117:1			Rom. 15:11	
118:6				Heb. 13:6
118:22		4:11		1 Peter 2:7
118:22–23	Matt. 21:42; Mark 12:10; Luke 20:17			

OT Passages	Gospels	Acts	Pauline Letters	General Letters
Ps. 118:26	Matt. 23:39; Luke 13:35			
140:3			Rom. 3:13	
Prov. 3:11–12				Heb. 12:5–6
3:34				James 4:6; 1 Peter 5:5
11:31				1 Peter 4:18
25:21–22			Rom. 12:20	
26:11				2 Peter 2:22
Isa. 1:9			Rom. 9:29	
6:9–10	Matt. 13:14–15; John 12:40	28:26–27		
7:14	Matt. 1:23			
8:14			Rom. 9:33	1 Peter 2:8
8:17 LXX				Heb. 2:13a
8:18				Heb. 2:13b
9:1f	Matt. 4:15–16			
10:22–23			Rom. 9:27–28	
11:10			Rom. 15:12	
12:3(?)	John 7:38			
22:13			1 Cor. 15:32	
25:8			1 Cor. 15:54–55	
26:19			Eph. 5:14	
27:9			Rom. 11:26–27	
28:11–12			1 Cor. 14:21	
28:16			Rom. 9:33; 10:11	1 Peter 2:6
29:10			Rom. 11:8	
29:13	Matt. 15:8–9; Mark 7:6–7			
29:14			1 Cor. 1:19	
40:3	Matt. 3:3; Mark 1:2–3			
40:3–5	Matt. 3:3; Mark 1:3; Luke 3:4–6; John 1:23			
40:6–8				1 Peter 1:24–25
40:13			Rom. 11:34–35; 1 Cor. 2:16	
42:1–4	Matt. 12:18–21			
45:23			Rom. 14:11	
49:6		13:47		
49:8			2 Cor. 6:2	
52:5			Rom. 2:24	
52:7			Rom. 10:15	
52:11–12			2 Cor. 6:16–18	
52:15			Rom. 15:21	
53:1	John 12:38		Rom. 10:16	
53:4	Matt. 8:17			
53:7–8		8:32–33		
53:12	Luke 22:37			
54:1			Gal. 4:27	
54:13	John 6:45			
55:3		13:34		
56:7	Matt. 21:13; Mark 11:17; Luke 19:46			

OT Passages	Gospels	Acts	Pauline Letters	General Letters
Isa. 58:6 58:11(?) 59:7–8 59:20–21 60:1 61:1–2 62:11(?) 64:4 65:1–2 66:1–2	Luke 4:18–19 John 7:38 Luke 4:18–19 Matt. 21:5	 7:49–50	 Rom. 3:15–17 Rom. 11:26–27 Eph. 5:14 1 Cor. 2:9 Rom. 10:20–21	
Jer. 7:11 9:24 31:15 31:31–34 31:33 31:34	Matt. 21:13; Mark 11:17; Luke 19:46 Matt. 2:18		 1 Cor. 1:31; 2 Cor. 10:17	 Heb. 8:8–12 Heb. 10:16 Heb. 10:17
Dan. 9:27 12:11	Matt. 24:15; Mark 13:14 Matt. 24:15; Mark 13:14			
Hos. 1:10 2:23 6:6 10:8 11:1 13:14	 Matt. 9:13; 12:7 Luke 23:30 Matt. 2:15		Rom. 9:26 Rom. 9:25 1 Cor. 15:54–55	
Joel 2:28–32 2:32		2:17–21	 Rom. 10:13	
Amos 5:25–27 9:11–12		7:42–43 15:16–18		
Hab. 1:5 2:3–4 2:4		13:41	 Rom. 1:17; Gal. 3:11	 Heb. 10:37–38
Hag. 2:6				Heb. 12:26
Zech. 9:9 11:12–13 12:10 13:7	Matt. 21:5; John 12:15 Matt. 27:9–10 John 19:37 Matt. 26:31; Mark 14:27			
Mal. 1:2–3 3:1	 Matt. 11:10; Mark 1:2–3; Luke 7:27		Rom. 9:13	

This list may not be exhaustive. Opinions differ in reference to individual citations in the NT as to whether the reference used by the NT author is a quotation or an allusion.

Selected New Testament Prophecies and Their Fulfillment in the New Testament Period

Prophecy—Scripture	Fulfillment—Scripture
"I will make you fishers of men." (Matt. 4:19; Mark 1:17)	Cf. Ministry of Christ; Acts (Matt. 28:19–20; Acts 1:8)
"The time will come when the bridegroom will be taken from them; then they will fast." (Matt. 9:15; Mark 2:20; Luke 5:35)	Ascension of Christ (Luke 24:50–51; Acts 1:9) Fasting of church (Acts 13:2–3; 14:23)
Suffering from religious leaders (Matt. 17:12) Death and resurrection (Matt. 16:21; 17:22–23; 20:18–19; Mark 8:31; 9:31; 10:32–34; Luke 9:22, 44; 18:31–33)	Passion accounts (Matt. 26–28; Mark 14–16; Luke 22–24; John 18–21)
"You will indeed drink from my cup." (Matt. 20:23; Mark 10:39)	Martyr death of James (Acts 12:1–2 c. A.D. 44)
"The Son of Man [came] … to give his life as a ransom for many." (Matt. 20:28; Mark 10:45)	Crucifixion (Matt. 27; Mark 15; Luke 23; John 19)
"Go to the village ahead of you, and at once you will find a donkey, … with her colt." (Matt. 21:2–3; Mark 11:2–3; Luke 19:30–31)	Matt. 21:6–7; Mark 11:4–6; Luke 19:32–34
"May you never bear fruit again!" (Matt. 21:18–19; Mark 11:12–14)	Assumed; cf. Matt. 21:19b
"The kingdom of God will be taken…." (Matt. 21:43–44)	Possibly the establishment of multiethnic church from Pentecost onward
"Not one stone here will be left on another…." (Matt. 24:2; Mark 13:2; Luke 21:6)	A.D. 70
"One of you will betray me." (Matt. 26:21, 23; Mark 14:18, 20; Luke 22:21; John 13:21, 26)	Betrayal by Judas (Matt. 26:14–16, 47–56; Mark 14:10–11, 43–50; Luke 22:3–6, 47–53; John 13:27; 18:3–12)

Prophecy—Scripture	Fulfillment—Scripture
"After I have risen I will go ahead of you into Galilee." (Matt. 26:32; Mark 14:28)	"He … is going ahead of you…." (Matt. 28:7, 10, 16; Mark 16:7)
"This very night, before the rooster crows, you will disown me." (Matt. 26:34; Mark 14:30; Luke 22:34; John 13:38)	Peter's denial (Matt. 26:69–75; Mark 14:66–72; Luke 22:54–62; John 18:15–18, 25–27)
"The demon has left your daughter." (Mark 7:29; cf. Matt. 15:28)	Mark 7:30
"She poured perfume on my body beforehand to prepare for my burial." (Matt. 26:12; Mark 14:8; John 12:7)	Burial (Matt. 27:57–61; Mark 15:42–47; Luke 23:50–56; John 19:38–42)
"Wherever the gospel is preached … what she has done will also be told." (Matt. 26:13; Mark 14:9)	Assumed
"Go into the city, and a man … will meet you." (Mark 14:13–15; Luke 22:10–12)	Passover preparation (Mark 14:16; Luke 22:13)
Zechariah foretells ministry of John the Baptist (Luke 1:67–79)	Ministry of John the Baptist (Matt. 3; Mark 1; Luke 3; John 1)
"Don't be afraid; just believe, and she will be healed." (Luke 8:50)	Restoration to life (Luke 8:55)
"Do not be afraid, little flock, for your Father has been pleased to give you the kingdom." (Luke 12:32)	Establishment of church
"The days will come upon you when your enemies will build … and encircle you." (Luke 19:43–44)	A.D. 66–70
"What is written about me is reaching its fulfillment." (Luke 22:37)	Crucifixion (Matt. 27:38; Mark 15:27; Luke 23:32–33; John 19:18)
"Today you will be with me in paradise." (Luke 23:43)	Assumed

Prophecy—Scripture	Fulfillment—Scripture
"Repentance and forgiveness of sins will be preached in his name to all nations." (Luke 24:47)	Cf. Acts 2
"I am going to send you what my Father has promised." (Luke 24:49)	Descent of the Holy Spirit (Acts 2:1–4)
"Destroy this temple, and I will raise it again in three days." (John 2:19–22)	Resurrection (Matt. 28:5–6; Mark 16:6; Luke 24:5–8; John 20:6–9)
"So the Son of Man must be lifted up." (John 3:14)	Crucifixion (Matt. 27; Mark 15; Luke 23; John 19)
"I lay down my life for the sheep.... I have authority to lay it down and authority to take it up again." (John 10:15–18)	Crucifixion and Resurrection (Matt. 27–28; Mark 15–16; Luke 23–24; John 19–21
Caiaphas: "It is better for you that one man die for the people." (John 11:49–50)	Crucifixion (Matt. 27; Mark 15; Luke 23; John 19; cf. John 11:51–52)
"The Father ... will give you another Counselor." (John 14:16, 23; 16:7)	Pentecost (Acts 2:1–4)
"I am returning to my Father." (John 20:17)	Ascension (Luke 24:50–51; Acts 1:9)
"When you are old ... someone else will ... lead you where you do not want to go." (John 21:18)	Martyrdom of Peter (cf. John 21:18–19, c. A.D. 64)
Promise of the Spirit (Acts 1:5–8)	Acts 2:1–4
Peter predicts Sapphira's death (Acts 5:9)	Acts 5:10
Agabus predicts famine (Acts 11:28)	Assumed (cf. Acts 11:29–30)
Paul's predictions to the Ephesian elders: 1. "None of you ... will ever see me again." (Acts 20:25) 2. False teachers without and within (Acts 20:29–30)	Assumed Assumed

Prophecy—Scripture	Fulfillment—Scripture
Agabus foretells Paul's arrest in Jerusalem (Acts 21:10–11)	Acts 21:33ff.
Paul predicts that all his shipmates will be preserved (Acts 27:22–25)	Acts 27:44

Prayers in the New Testament

Gospels
Synoptic Parallels

The Lord's prayer—Matt. 6:9–13; Luke 11:2–4

Leper's prayer for healing (Ch)[1] —Matt. 8:2; Mark 1:40; Luke 5:12

Jesus prays in the desert—Mark 1:35; Luke 5:16

Centurion's prayer (Ch)—Matt. 8:6, 8; Luke 7:6–7

Prayer for calming storm (Ch)—Matt. 8:25; Mark 4:38; Luke 8:24

Prayer of Gadarene demoniac(s) (Ch)—Matt. 8:29; Mark 5:7; Luke 8:28

Prayer of Gadarene demons (Ch)—Matt. 8:31; Mark 5:9–12; Luke 8:30–32

Jairus's prayer (Ch)—Matt. 9:18; Mark 5:22–23; Luke 8:41–42

Jesus' thanksgiving to the Father—Matt. 11:25–26; Luke 10:21

Blessing at feeding of 5,000—Matt. 14:19; Mark 6:41; Luke 9:16; cf. John 6:11

Jesus' prayer on the mountain—Matt. 14:23; Mark 6:46

Prayer of a foreign woman (Ch)—Matt. 15:21–28; Mark 7:24–30

Blessing at feeding of 4,000—Matt. 15:36; Mark 8:6

Prayer for moonstruck (demoniac) (Ch)—Matt. 17:14–15; Mark 9:17–18; Luke 9:38–40

Prayer of the blind man at Jericho (Ch)—Matt. 20:30–33; Mark 10:47–51; Luke 18:38–41

Blessing of Lord's Supper—Matt. 26:26–27; Mark 14:22–23; Luke 22:17–19

Jesus' prayer in Gethsemane—Matt. 26:36–46; Mark 14:32–42; Luke 22:39–46

Prayer on the cross—Matt. 27:46; Mark 15:34; Luke 23:46

Other References to Prayer in the Gospels

Prayer of blind men (Ch)—Matt. 9:27–28

Peter's prayer on the water (Ch)—Matt. 14:30

Jesus prays for a deaf and dumb man—Mark 7:34

Prayer of Simeon in the temple—Luke 2:29–32

Jesus' prayer at baptism—Luke 3:21

Jesus' prayer before choosing apostles—Luke 6:12–13

Jesus' prayer on Mount of Transfiguration—Luke 9:28–29

Prayer of ten lepers (Ch)—Luke 17:12–13

Jesus' prayer for Peter's faith—Luke 22:31–32

Blessing of food on Emmaus journey—Luke 24:30

Prayer of nobleman for his son—John 4:47, 49

Jesus' prayer at Lazarus's tomb—John 11:41–42

Jesus' prayer answered by the Father—John 12:27–28

Jesus' great prayer—John 17

[1] (Ch) = prayer addressed to Christ

Acts
Disciples' prayer in the upper room—1:13–14
Prayer for successor to Judas—1:24–25
Peter and John go to temple at hour of prayer—3:1
Prayer for boldness in witnessing—4:24–31
Prayer in choosing first deacons—6:6
Stephen's final prayer—7:59–60
Peter and John's prayer for Samaritans—8:14–17
Saul's prayer at conversion (Ch)—9:5, 11
Ananias's vision—9:10, 13–14
Peter's prayer for Dorcas—9:40
Cornelius's prayer and vision—10:1–8
Peter's prayer and vision in Joppa—10:9–16
Prayer for Peter in prison—12:5, 12
Prayer for commissioning of Saul and Barnabas—13:3
Prayer for ordaining elders—14:23
Riverside prayer meeting in Macedonia—16:13, 16
Paul and Silas pray in Philippian jail—16:25
Paul's prayer with Ephesian elders—20:36
Paul's prayer outside of Tyre—21:5
Paul's prayer at Temple—22:17
Paul blesses food on Roman voyage—27:35
Paul's prayer for Publius's father—28:8

Epistles	
Romans	Paul prays that he might see the Romans—1:8–12 Prayer for Israel's salvation—10:1 Benedictions—15:33; 16:20 Doxology—16:25–27
1 Corinthians	Thanksgiving for richness of spiritual gifts—1:4–9
2 Corinthians	Blessing of God—1:3–7 Benediction—13:14
Galatians	Benediction—6:18
Ephesians	Blessing of God for His blessings—1:3–14 Prayer for knowledge and power—1:15–21 Prayer for strength, indwelling, and understanding—3:14–19 Doxology—3:20–21 Benediction—6:24

Philippians	Prayer for understanding and love—1:2–11 Doxology—4:20 Benediction—4:23
Colossians	Prayer for growth of the gospel—1:3–6 Prayer for wisdom and understanding—1:9–12 Benediction—4:18
1 Thessalonians	Thanksgiving for God's choice—1:2–5 Prayer for return visit—3:9–13 Prayer for thorough sanctification—5:23–24 Benediction—5:28
2 Thessalonians	Thanksgiving for love and faith—1:3 Prayer for worthiness of calling—1:11–12 Thanksgiving and prayer for calling and establishment—2:13–17 Prayer for peace—3:16 Benediction—3:18
1 Timothy	Thanksgiving and doxology for God's mercy—1:12–17 Benediction—6:21
2 Timothy	Thanksgiving for Timothy's faith—1:3–5 Prayer for Onesiphorus—1:16–18 Prayer for judgment on Alexander—4:14 Doxology—4:18 Benediction—4:22
Titus	Benediction—3:15
Philemon	Benediction—v. 25
1 Peter	Blessing of God for a living hope and incorruptible inheritance—1:3–4 Doxology—4:11 Prayer for stability/doxology—5:10–11 Benediction—5:14
2 Peter	Doxology—3:18
3 John	Prayer for Gaius's health—v. 2
Jude	Benediction—vv. 24–25
Revelation	Doxology—1:6 Prayer of martyrs—6:10 Prayer of gentile multitude—7:9–12 Prayer of twenty-four elders—11:16–18 "Amen. Come, Lord Jesus." (Ch)—22:20

Sermons and Speeches in the New Testament

Gospels
Preaching of John the Baptist—Matt. 3:2, 7–12 (Mark 1:7–8; Luke 3:7–9, 16–18)
Sermon on the Mount—Matt. 5–7
Sermon at commissioning of the Twelve—Matt. 10:5–42
Controversy over casting out demons—Matt. 12:22–45
The parable—Matt. 13:1–52 (Mark 4:1–34; Luke 8:4–18)
Sermon on tradition/elders—Matt. 15:1–20 (Mark 7:1–23)
Denunciation of Scribes and Pharisees—Matt. 23
(Olivet Discourse) Last Days—Matt. 24:4–25:46 (Mark 13:3–37; Luke 21:7–36)
Simeon's speech to Mary and Joseph—Luke 2:28–35
Jesus' first sermon in synagogue—Luke 4:17–27
Sermon on the plain—Luke 6:17–49
Sermon on the lost—Luke 15
Sermon on authority of the Son—John 5:19–47
Bread of Life discourse—John 6:22–59
Jesus' sermon at Feast of Tabernacles—John 7:37–38
Sermon on sheep and shepherd—John 10:1–18
Sermon in the Upper Room—John 13:31–16:33

Acts
Peter's speech at selection of Judas's successor—1:16–22
Peter's sermon on Day of Pentecost—2:14–36
Peter's sermon in Solomon's Colonnade—3:12–26
Peter's speech before the council—4:8–12
Gamaliel's speech before the council—5:35–39
Stephen's sermon before the council—7:2–53
Peter's sermon in Cornelius's house—10:34–43
Peter's defense to the church in Jerusalem—11:4–17
Peter's sermon in the synagogue at Antioch of Pisidia—13:16–41
Paul and Barnabas appeal in Lystra—14:15–17
Peter's speech at Jerusalem council—15:7–11
James's speech at Jerusalem council—15:13–21
Paul's speech in Athens—17:22–31
Demetrius's speech in the Ephesian theater—19:25–27
Paul's farewell message to Ephesian elders—20:18–35
Paul's defense before the mob—22:1–21
Paul's defense before the council—23:1–6
Paul's defense before Felix—24:10–21
Paul's defense before Festus—25:8, 10–11
Paul's defense before Agrippa—26:1–23
Paul's speech to his shipmates—27:21–26
Paul's testimony to Jews in Rome—28:17–20, 25–28

Old Testament Characters in the New Testament

Aaron	Brother of Moses; in Stephen's speech (Acts 7:40); example of old levitical order superseded by Christ (Heb. 5:4; 7:11); rod contained in covenant box (Heb. 9:4).
Abel	Brother of Cain; avenging of his blood (Matt. 23:35; Luke 11:51); example of faith (Heb. 11:4); Jesus' blood speaks better things than his (Heb. 12:24).
Abiathar	Priest during time of David's wanderings (Mark 2:26).
Abraham	Traditional father of the Jews (Matt. 3:9; Luke 13:16; 19:9; John 8:33–58; Acts 7:2–8; 2 Cor. 11:22; Heb. 2:16); entertaining Gentiles in the kingdom of heaven (Matt. 8:11; cf. Luke 13:28); received the promises (Luke 1:55, 73; Acts 3:25; Gal. 4:22; Heb. 6:13); received Lazarus in parable of rich man (Luke 16:22–30); mentioned in "Salvation History" sermon by Stephen (Acts 7:2–8); blessed by Melchizedek (Heb. 7:1–10); example of justification by faith (Rom. 4:1–22; Gal. 3:6–29); example of faith (Heb. 11:8–11, 17–19); example of good works (James 2:21, 23); wife Sarah submitted to him (1 Peter 3:6).
Adam	The "first man" through whom sin and death came into the world (Rom. 5:12–21); the "earthly" man contrasted to the heavenly, resurrected Christ (1 Cor. 15:22, 45–49); formed first and not deceived by the serpent (1 Tim. 2:13–14).
Balaam	The "way" and "error" of Balaam, who loved the wages of unrighteousness (2 Peter 2:15; Jude 11); the "doctrine" of Balaam, associated with idolatry and fornication (Rev. 2:14).
Barak	Example of faith (Heb. 11:32).
Cain	Abel's faith offering more acceptable than his (Heb. 11:4); murder of Abel example of evil (1 John 3:12); false teachers follow the "way" of Cain (Jude 11).
David	Ate bread intended for priests only (Matt. 12:3–4; Mark 2:25–26; Luke 6:3–4); called the Messiah Lord (Matt. 22:42–45; Mark 12:35–37; Luke 20:41–44); Messiah born in his city (Luke 2:11); died but did not ascend into heaven (Acts 2:29, 34); man after God's own heart (Acts 13:22); died and saw corruption (Acts 13:36); Christ of his seed according to the flesh (Rom. 1:3; 2 Tim. 2:8); example of faith (Heb. 11:32); Jesus has the key of David (Rev. 3:7); Jesus the Root of David (Rev. 5:5; 22:16).
Elijah	Identified with John the Baptist (Matt. 11:14; Luke 1:17; John 1:21, 25); identified with Jesus (Matt. 16:14; Mark 8:28; Luke 9:19); appeared on Mount of Transfiguration with Jesus and Moses (Matt. 17:3–13; Mark 9:2–8; Luke 9:28–36); some thought Jesus on the cross called him (Matt. 27:47–49; Mark 15:35); sent to widow of Zarephath (Luke 4:25–26); man of prayer (James 5:17).

Elisha	Cleansed Naaman the Syrian (Luke 4:27).
Enoch	Translated by faith (Heb. 11:5); credited with prophecy concerning false prophets (Jude 14).
Esau	Father's blessing and prophecy by faith (Heb. 11:20); condemned for selling his birthright (Heb. 12:16).
Eve	Formed after Adam, deceived by serpent (1 Tim. 2:13–14; 2 Cor. 11:3).
Gabriel	Angel; announced births of John the Baptist and Jesus (Luke 1:19, 26).
Hagar	Cited as allegorical representation of Mosaic covenant (Gal. 4:24–25).
Isaac	Entertaining Gentiles in kingdom of heaven (Matt. 8:11; cf. Luke 13:28); among the chosen (Acts 7:8); example of God's selection (Rom. 9:7, 10); Galatian Christians children of Isaac's promise (Gal. 4:28); example of faith and of works (James 2:21); father offered him (Heb. 11:17–19); blessed Jacob and Esau (Heb. 11:20).
Jacob	Entertaining Gentiles in kingdom of heaven (Matt. 8:11; cf. Luke 13:28); traditional father of Israelites (John 4:12); his well in Samaria (John 4:5–6); among the chosen (Acts 7:8, 12); example of God's selection (Rom. 9:13); by faith blessed Joseph's sons (Heb. 11:21).
Jannes and Jambres	Two of Pharaoh's magicians; opposed Moses (2 Tim. 3:8).[1]
Jephthah	Example of faith (Heb. 11:32).
Jeremiah	Identified with Jesus (Matt. 16:14).
Jezebel	Name given to a woman who lured Christians to fornication and idolatry (Rev. 2:20).[2]
Job	Example of patience (James 5:11).
Jonah	Parallel with Jesus in His death and resurrection (Matt. 12:39–40; 16:4; Luke 11:29–30) and His preaching (Matt. 12:41; Luke 11:32).
Joseph	Plot of ground in Samaria given him by his father (John 4:5); mentioned in "Salvation History" sermon by Stephen (Acts 7:9–18); example of faith (Heb. 11:22).
Joshua	Mentioned in "Salvation History" sermon by Stephen (Acts 7:45–46); did not give rest to Israel by entering Canaan (Heb. 4:8).
Korah	False teachers perished in the dispute of Korah (Jude 11).
Levi	Paid tithes to Melchizedek through Abraham (Heb. 7:5–10).

[1] Do not appear by name in the Old Testament. Their names are found in traditions.

[2] Not the actual Jezebel from the Old Testament. Her name is used allegorically.

Lot	Mentioned in connection with God's judgment on Sodom and Gomorrah (Luke 17:28–29; 2 Peter 2:7).
Melchizedek	Order of Jesus' priesthood (Heb. 5, 7).
Michael	Archangel; disputed with the devil about the body of Moses (Jude 9); war against the dragon in heaven (Rev. 12:7).
Moses	Lawgiver (multiple references); appeared on Mount of Transfiguration with Jesus and Elijah (Matt. 17:3–4; Mark 9:4–5; Luke 9:30, 33); scribes and Pharisees sit in Moses' seat (Matt. 23:2); wrote about Christ (Luke 24:27; John 5:45–46); religious leaders claimed to be his disciples (John 9:28–29); prophesied the Messiah (Acts 3:22; 26:22); was remarkably called by God, then led Israelites out of Egypt, as mentioned in "Salvation History" sermon by Stephen (Acts 7:20–44); Paul accused of teaching apostasy from Moses (Acts 21:21); children of Israel baptized into Moses (1 Cor. 10:2); Jannes and Jambres opposed him (2 Tim. 3:8); a servant of God but inferior to the Son (Heb. 3:1–6); example of faith (Heb. 11:23–24); Michael and the devil disputed over his body (Jude 9); Song of Moses coupled with song of the Lamb (Rev. 15:3).
Naaman	Gentile leper healed by Elisha (Luke 4:27).
Noah	Associated with judgment of the Flood (Matt. 24:37–38; Luke 17:26–27; 1 Peter 3:20); example of faith (Heb. 11:7); preacher of righteousness (2 Peter 2:5).
Pharaoh	Moses refused to be called the son of Pharaoh's daughter (Heb. 11:24).
Queen of the South (Sheba)	Came a great distance to hear Solomon (Matt. 12:42; Luke 11:31).
Rahab	Example of faith (Heb. 11:31); of works (James 2:25).
Rebecca	Mother of Jacob and Esau (Rom. 9:10).
Samson	Example of faith (Heb. 11:32).
Samuel	Classed among the prophets (Acts 3:24; 13:20); example of faith (Heb. 11:32).
Saul	King of Israel; given and removed by God (Acts 13:21–22).
Solomon	Not dressed like the flowers (Matt. 6:29; Luke 12:27); Queen of the South came to hear him (Matt. 12:42; Luke 11:31); his Colonnade (NIV usage) in the Temple (John 10:23; Acts 3:11; 5:12); builder of the Temple, as mentioned in "Salvation History" sermon by Stephen (Acts 7:47).
Zechariah	His blood to be required of (Jesus') generation (Matt. 23:35; Luke 11:51).

Prominent Secondary Figures of the New Testament

Name	Personal Information	Scripture
Ananias/ Sapphira	Lied to the Holy Spirit by retaining a portion of the purchase price of their land. Were disciplined with death.	Acts 5:1–5
Apollos	Named after the Greek god or possibly a contraction of Apollonius or Apollodorus. He was a Jew from Alexandria who was learned and eloquent in the Scriptures. Originally he knew only the baptism of John. Ministered in Ephesus and Corinth. In the latter some favored him over Paul.	Acts 18:24–28; 19:1; 1 Cor. 1:12; 3:4–6, 22; 4:6; 16:12; Titus 3:13
Aquila and Priscilla	Jews from Pontus who came to Corinth from Rome, probably when Claudius expelled all Jews in c. A.D. 49. Were tentmakers with whom Paul later worked to support himself. Instructed Apollos concerning Jesus. Accompanied Paul to Ephesus; returned to Rome and later went back to Ephesus. Were hosts of a house-church.	Acts 18:1–3, 18–19, 26; Rom. 16:3–5a; 1 Cor. 16:19; 2 Tim. 4:19
Barnabas	Name means "son of exhortation/consolation." Jew from Cyprus and a Levite. Sold property for alms. Teacher at Antioch with Saul. Companion with Saul/Paul on first missionary journey. Parted company with Paul over dispute concerning Mark, with whom he went to Cyprus while Paul took Silas as a partner for second missionary journey.	Acts 4:36–37; 9:27; 11:22–30; 12:25; 13:1–14:28; 15:1–40; 1 Cor. 9:6; Gal. 2:1, 9, 13; Col. 4:10
Herod Antipas	Tetrarch of Galilee and Perea (4 B.C.–A.D. 39) and son of Herod the Great. Had John the Baptist beheaded. Built Tiberias, his capital. Married and divorced daughter of Nabatean king, Aretas, in order to marry Herodias, wife of his brother Philip. Aretas avenged his daughter with an invasion. Is Herod of the Passion narratives.	Matt. 14:1–12; Mark 6:14–29; Luke 3:19–20; 8:3; 9:7–9; 23:7–12; Acts 4:27; 13:1
Herod the Great	Built temple in Jerusalem. Ruler of all the Jewish territories as king. Built many palace fortresses, including Antonia in Jerusalem, summer palace near Bethlehem, and Masada. Slaughtered children two years and under in Bethlehem to do away with any rival. Notoriously jealous, had several members of his family killed whom he saw as possible rivals. Able politician and ruler and in favor with Rome. Son of Antipater the Idumean. (37 B.C.–4 B.C.)	Matt. 2:1–23; Luke 1:5

Name	Personal Information	Scripture
John the Baptist	A cousin of Jesus born to priest Zechariah and wife, Elizabeth, who had been childless. A prophet and messenger to prepare the way of the Lord. Preached a baptism of repentance. Was imprisoned and beheaded by Herod Antipas. Had disciples to continue his ministry even after the coming of Messiah, as far as Ephesus.	Matt. 3; 4:12; 9:14; 11:2–18; 14:2–10; 16:14; 17:13; 21:25–32; Mark 1:4–14; 2:18; 6:14–29; 11:27–32; Luke 1:13–80; 3:2–20; 7:18–35; 9:7, 19; 11:1; 16:16; 20:4–6; John 1:6–40; 3:23–36; 4:1; 5:33–36; 10:40–41; Acts 1:5, 22; 10:37; 11:16; 13:24–25; 19:4
Joseph, Husband of Mary	Engaged to Mary at the time of the conception and birth of Jesus. Called a "just" man. Took Mary and Jesus to Egypt after warned by an angel that Herod desired to kill the child. Lived in Nazareth and was a carpenter. Was a descendant of David the king. Legal, but not physical, parent of Jesus.	Matt. 1:16–25; 2:13–15; Luke 1:27; 2:4–51; 3:23; 4:22; John 1:45; 6:42
Lazarus of Bethany	Brother of Mary and Martha who was raised from the dead by Jesus. Religious leaders wished to kill him. A close friend of Christ. Should not be identified with the Lazarus of Luke 16:19–31.	John 11:1–44; 12:2, 9–10, 17
Luke	Gentile author of Luke–Acts who was a close friend of Paul the apostle. Traveled with Paul on second and third missionary journeys and the voyage to Rome. Called the "beloved physician." Hometown perhaps Antioch or Philippi.	Luke 1:1–4; Acts 1:1; 16:10–18; 20:5–21:18; 27:1–28:16; Col. 4:14; Philem. 24; 2 Tim. 4:11
Mark	Cousin of Barnabas whose Jewish name was John and Latin name was Mark. Lived in Jerusalem. Started on first missionary journey with Barnabas and Saul but deserted them after they reached the southern coast of Asia(?). Went with Barnabas to Cyprus to encourage the new Christians there while Paul and Silas went on second missionary journey. With Paul in Rome and Peter in "Babylon," probably Rome. A writer of a gospel, possibly for Peter. Mother's name was Mary.	Acts 12:12, 25; 13:5, 13; 15:36–39; Col. 4:10; 2 Tim. 4:11; Philem. 24; 1 Peter 5:13
Mary of Bethany	Sister of Lazarus and Martha. Anointed Jesus' feet at a supper and sat at His feet for His teaching.	Luke 10:38–42; John 11:1–44; 12:1–8

Name	Personal Information	Scripture
Mary, Mother of Jesus	Betrothed to Joseph and virgin mother of Jesus according to an announcement by the angel Gabriel. Visited her cousin Elizabeth with great rejoicing. Urged Jesus to provide wine at wedding at Cana. Remained at the Crucifixion after the disciples had fled. Given into the hands of John the beloved by Jesus before He died. Has received special praise by the church through the centuries.	Matt. 1–2; Mark 6:3; Luke 1–2; John 19:26; Acts 1:14
Mary Magdalene	First to see the resurrected Lord. Was from Magdala on the northwest shore of Sea of Galilee. Delivered by Jesus from seven demons. One of the women at the Crucifixion and burial. Met the angel who announced the Resurrection. Contributed to Jesus' and disciples' support.	Matt. 27:56–61; 28:1; Mark 15:40–47; 16:1–9; Luke 8:2; 24:10; John 19:25; 20:1–18
Nicodemus	Pharisee and member of Sanhedrin. Came to Jesus by night and received teaching from Jesus on being born again. Defended Jesus in the council and helped Joseph of Arimathea with burial preparations.	John 3:1–9; 7:50; 19:39
Pontius Pilate	Roman prefect of Judea, Idumea, and Samaria (A.D. 26–36) appointed by Tiberius. He moved the military headquarters from Caesarea to Jerusalem. His actions agitated the Jews who often complained to Rome (including the slaughter of Galileans, Luke 13:1). Driven by political pressure (in view of his action of taking temple funds to build aqueducts in Jerusalem among other things) to deliver Jesus over to be crucified. After putting down a Samaritan revolt, was sent to Rome on charge of maladministration.	Matt. 27; Mark 15; Luke 3:1; 13:1; 23:1–52; John 18–19; Acts 3:13; 4:27; 13:28; 1 Tim. 6:13
Silas	A Roman citizen whose Latin name was Silvanus. He brought a letter from the Jerusalem Council to Antioch. Was a prophet, accompanied Paul on his second missionary journey, was jailed at Philippi with Paul, and was Peter's amanuensis in the writing of his first epistle.	Acts 15:22, 27, 32–34, 40–41; 16:1–17:15; 18:5; 2 Cor. 1:19; 1 Thess. 1:1; 2 Thess. 1:1; 1 Peter 5:12
Timothy	Greek = "honoring God." Paul's spiritual son and helper for about fifteen to twenty years. Subject to frequent sickness. His hometown was Lystra and he had a Greek father but a Jewish mother and grandmother. Accompanied Paul on his second missionary journey, was ordained by elders, was with Paul in his Roman imprisonment, and was chosen by the apostle as a legate to care for the church at Ephesus.	Acts 16:1–3; 17:14–15; 18:5; 19:22; 20:4; Rom. 16:21; 1 Cor. 4:17; 16:10–11; 2 Cor. 1:1, 19; Phil. 1:1; 2:19–23; Col. 1:1; 1 Thess. 1:1; 3:2, 6; 2 Thess. 1:1; 1 Tim. 1:2, 18; 6:20; 2 Tim. 1:2; 4:9, 21; Philem. 1; Heb. 13:23
Titus	Went with Paul on a trip to Jerusalem and coworker at Ephesus. Helped to carry the offering to Jerusalem. Left as a legate in Crete to care for the churches there and finally in Dalmatia.	2 Cor. 2:12–13; 7:7, 13–14; 8:6, 16–17, 23; 12:17–18; Gal. 2:1–3; Titus 1:5; 2 Tim. 4:10

PART II
Backgrounds to the New Testament

A Chronological History of Rome

Dates[1]	Events	Persons
600 B.C.	Overthrow of Etruscan control at Rome and the founding of the republic (509) First consuls appointed (508) First dictator (501)	
500	Alliance of Rome and the Latins (493) Twelve Tables (451–450)	
400	Rome captured by the Gauls (390) First Samnite War (343–341) The Latin War (340–338) Dissolution of Latin League (338) Second Samnite War (328–302)	
300	Third Samnite War (298–290) First Punic War (264–241) Roman envoys in Athens and Corinth (228) Second Punic War (218–201) Hannibal's crossing of the Alps (218) First Macedonian War (214–205) Rome's defeat of Carthage at Zama (202)	Cato the Elder (234–149)
200	Second Macedonian War: Rome's defeat of Philip V (200–196) Repeal of Oppian Law (195) War with Antiochus III (the Great) (192–189) Third Macedonian War (171–168) Voconian Law (169) Third Punic War: Carthage destroyed (149–146) War with the Achaeans: Corinth destroyed (146)	
100	Slave war in Sicily (139–132) Slave war with Spartacus (73–71) First consulship of Pompey and Crassus (70) Pompey's capture of Jerusalem (63) Consulship of Cicero (63) Coalition of Pompey, Caesar, and Crassus (60) First consulship of Caesar (59) Caesar's Gallic Wars (58–51)	Cicero (106–43) Cato the Younger (95–46) Catullus (84–54) Virgil (70–19) Horace (65–8) Lucretius (60) Livy (59 B.C.–A.D. 17)

[1] Dates are approximate, most within 1–2 years due to variation in reckoning methods.

Dates[1]	Events	Persons
100 B.C.	Cicero exiled (58) Cicero recalled (57) Second consulship of Pompey and Crassus (55) Caesar's invasions of Britain (55–54) Crassus defeated and killed by the Parthians (53) Pompey sole consul (52) Julius Caesar's defeat of Pompey at Pharsalus (49) Caesar's dictatorship (49–44) Assassination of Julius Caesar (March 15, 44) Octavian consul and Antony, Lepidus, and Octavian triumvirs (43) Octavian and Mark Antony's defeat of Brutus and Cassius at Philippi (42) Defeat of Sextus Pompey (36) Parthian War (36) Death of Antony and Cleopatra VIII, and the annexation of Egypt (30) Octavian Augustus Caesar (27 B.C.–A.D. 14) Annexation of Galatia (25)	Ovid (43 B.C.–A.D. 17)
1 B.C.–A.D.1	Campaigns against Germanicus (14–17) Tiberius (14–37)	Seneca (4? B.C.–A.D. 65) Pliny the Elder (23–79)
	Caligula (37–41)	Lucan (39–65) Martial (40–104)
	Claudius (41–54) Invasion and annexation of southern Britain (43) Nero (54–68) Assassination of Agrippina, mother of Nero (59) Fire in Rome; Christians persecuted (64) Vespasian (69–79) Destruction of Jerusalem (70)	Juvenal (50s–after 127) Tacitus (55–129?) Pliny the Younger (61–112) Suetonius (69–140)
	Titus (79–81) Destruction of Pompeii and Herculaneum (79) Domitian (81–96) Trajan (98–117) Hadrian (117–38) Revolt of the Jews in the East (132–35) Final Jewish revolt against Rome put down (135)	

A Chronological History of Greece

Dates	Events	Persons
600 B.C.	Peloponnesian league founded (c. 550)	Solon, the Archon (594) Anaximander Anaximenes
	Tyranny of Athens (c. 546)	
	Democracy at Athens (507)	Pythagoras Xenophanes Heraclitus
500	Ionian revolt (499–493) Persian attack on Athens (490) Persian attack of Greek (480–479) Athenian alliance founded (478)	Pindar
		Lysias (459–380) Aeschylus (458)
	Citizenship Law of Pericles (451–450) Athens's peace with Persia (448)	
	Peloponnesian War (431–404)	Sophocles (441) Herodotus Anaxagoras Hippocrates Socrates Aristophanes (431) Plato (429–380) Xenophon (428–354) Demosthenes Aristotle (d. 322) Euripides (d. 405)
400	Expedition of the 10,000 (401–400) Spartan expedition in Asia Minor (400–394) Sparta's peace with Persia (386) Thebes's defeat of Sparta (371)	
		Menander (342–291) Epicurus (341–271)

Dates	Events	Persons
300	Philip II of Macedon conquers Greece (338) Alexander's attack on Persia (334) Death of Alexander (323) Beginning of Seleucid Era (311) First Syrian War (274–271) Second Syrian War (260–253) Third Syrian War (246–241) Antiochus III (the Great), Seleucid ruler of Syria (223–187) Antiochus III driven from Egypt; defeated at Raphia by Ptolemy IV (217)	Zeno (336–264) Aratus of Soli (315–240)
200	Antiochus III's defeat of Egypt at battle of Panium and control of Palestine (198) Seleucids driven from Asia Minor by Romans (188) Syro-Palestine ruled by Antiochus IV (Epiphanes) (175–164) Antiochus's attack on Jerusalem and persecution of the Jews (168) Maccabean revolt against the Syrians (167) Syria's loss of political control over Judea (142)	Polybius (208–126)

A Chronological History of Israel

Dates[1]	Events	Persons
600 B.C.	Jerusalem destroyed by Nebuchadnezzar (587) Cyrus's defeat of Media (549) Babylon's fall to Cyrus (539) Darius I ruler of Persian Empire (522–486)	
	Second temple in Jerusalem completed (515)	Haggai (520) Zechariah (520)
500		
	Xerxes I's rule (486–464) Artaxerxes I's rule (464–423)	Esther Nehemiah Malachi (450) Ezra (c. 400)
400		
	Samaritan schism; Samaritan temple built on Mt. Gerizim Alexander's conquering of Palestine (c. 330) Control of Judah by Ptolemy I (Soter) (323–285)	
300		
	Translation of the Pentateuch into Greek (LXX) under Ptolemy II (c. 250) Capture of Jerusalem by Antiochus III (203)	
200		
	Palestine under Seleucid control (198) Antiochus IV (Epiphanes) king of Syria (175–164) Jerusalem made a Hellenistic city (172) Antiochus IV forced by Rome to withdraw from Egypt (168) Persecution of the Jews begun by Antiochus and "abomination of desolation" set up in temple (December 168) Maccabean Revolt (167) Jews' defeat of Syria at Beth-Zur rededication of temple (December 164)	Mattathias (d. 166) Hasmonean
	Death of Antiochus IV (163) Judas's siege of Syrian garrison in Jerusalem (163–162)	Judas Hasmonean (Maccabeus) (d. 161) Jonathan (d. 142)
	Jonathan's succession to Judas (158–142) Simon's succession to Jonathan (142–135) Jewish independence gained (142) Judean independence recognized by Roman senate (139) John Hyrcanus's succession to Simon (135–105) Emergence of the Pharisees and Sadducees for the first time (c. 135) Destruction of the Samaritan temple on Mt. Gerizim by John Hyrcanus (109–108)	Simon (d. 135)

[1] Variations exist in the dates listed, reflecting different methods of reckoning.

Dates[1]	Events	Persons
100		
	Civil war, Aristobulus II vs. Hyrcanus II in Judea (67–63)	
	Pompey's conquering of Jerusalem (63)	
	Hyrcanus II installed as ruler (63)	
	Antipater governor of Judea (47)	
	Herod governor of Galilee (47)	
	Herod crowned king of the Jews (40)	
	Invasion of Syria and Palestine by Parthians (40)	
	Parthians driven out; Herod's assumption of kingdom (37–34)	
	Rebuilding of temple begun by Herod (20)	
	Building of Caesarea completed by Herod (10)	
	Death of Herod the Great (4)	
	Archelaus, ethnarch of Judea, Samaria, and Idumea (4 B.C.–A.D. 6)	
1 B.C.–A.D. 1		
	Judea made a Roman imperial province Jewish uprising (7)	
	Founding of Tiberias (23)	
	Pilate's arrival in Judea (26)	Pilate (26–36)
	Pilate dismissed as prefect of Judea (36)	
	Birth of Josephus (37)	Josephus (37–c. 95)
	Anti-Jewish riots in Alexandria (38)	
	Herod Antipas exiled (39)	
	Anti-Jewish riots in Antioch (40)	
	A group of Alexandrian Jews led by Philo to Caligula	
	Death of Herod Agrippa I (44)	
	Rise of the Zealots and Sicarii (50–52)	
	Josephus's pleading of Jewish interests before Nero (64)	Paul (d. 64–68)
	Jewish revolt against Rome (66–70)	Peter (d. 64–68)
	Josephus's surrender to Vespasian (67)	
	Fall of Jerusalem (70)	
	Fall of Masada (73)	
	Josephus's completion of *Jewish War* (75–79)	
	Josephus's completion of *Antiquities* (93–94)	
	Synod of Jamnia (90?)	John (d. 100)
	Jewish revolt of Bar-Cochba (132–135)	
	Final Jewish revolt against Rome put down and Jerusalem made a Gentile city (135)	
	Martyrdom of Rabban Akiba (135?)	

The Structure of Roman Society

Emperor

Proconsul, Propraetor, Legate Consul,

Praetor, Prefect (equestrian)

(patrician) Quaestor, Aedil, Tribune (plebian)

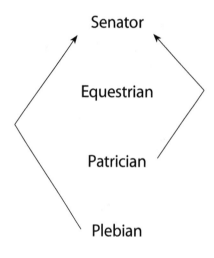

Senator

Equestrian

Patrician

Plebian

Freedman

Slave

Arrows indicate possibility or likelihood of upward mobility.

Adapted from Merland Ray Miller, "Timetables and Charts for the New Testament," ThM thesis (Portland, Ore.: Western Conservative Baptist Seminary, 1980), by permission.

The Roman Political System

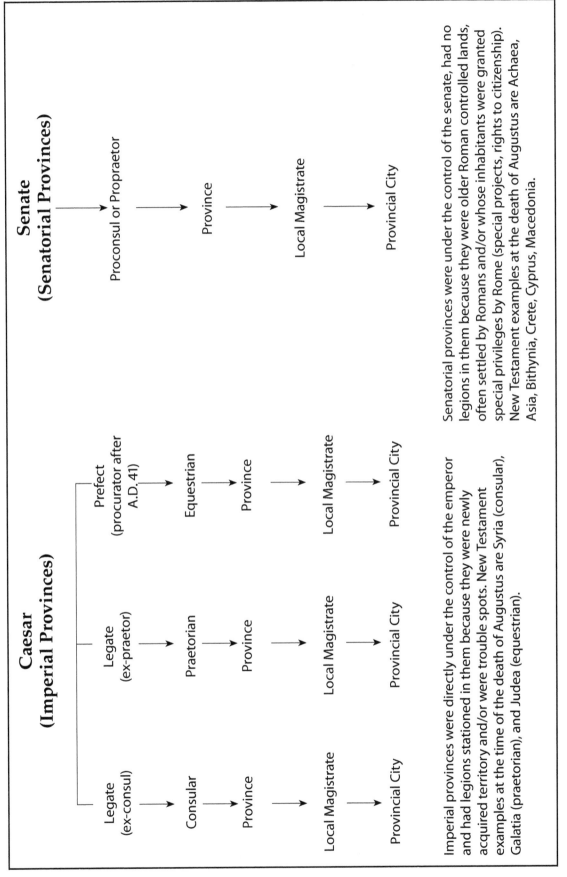

Caesar (Imperial Provinces)

Legate (ex-consul) → Consular → Province → Local Magistrate → Provincial City

Legate (ex-praetor) → Praetorian → Province → Local Magistrate → Provincial City

Prefect (procurator after A.D. 41) → Equestrian → Province → Local Magistrate → Provincial City

Senate (Senatorial Provinces)

Proconsul or Propraetor → Province → Local Magistrate → Provincial City

Imperial provinces were directly under the control of the emperor and had legions stationed in them because they were newly acquired territory and/or were trouble spots. New Testament examples at the time of the death of Augustus are Syria (consular), Galatia (praetorian), and Judea (equestrian).

Senatorial provinces were under the control of the senate, had no legions in them because they were older Roman controlled lands, often settled by Romans and/or whose inhabitants were granted special privileges by Rome (special projects, rights to citizenship). New Testament examples at the death of Augustus are Achaea, Asia, Bithynia, Crete, Cyprus, Macedonia.

Adapted from Merland Ray Miller, "Timetables and Charts for the New Testament," ThM thesis (Portland, Ore.: Western Conservative Baptist Seminary, 1980), by permission.

The Roman Military System

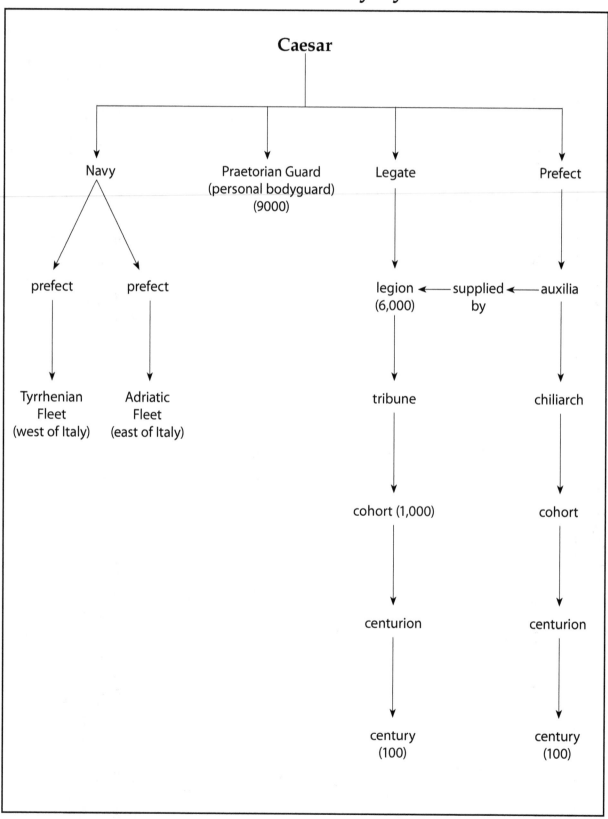

Adapted from Merland Ray Miller, "Timetables and Charts for the New Testament," ThM thesis (Portland, Ore.: Western Conservative Baptist Seminary, 1980), by permission.

Graeco-Roman Deities

Greek Name	Roman Name	Position	Scripture Reference
Aphrodite	Venus	Goddess of love	
Apollo	Sol (also identified with Helios)	Shepherd-god; sun-god; associated with poetry, music, prophecy, and hunting	
Ares	Mars	War-god; also linked with agriculture; Areopagus (Mars Hill) named after him	Acts 17:22
Artemis	Diana	Goddess of fertility	Acts 19:21–40
Asklepios (Asclepius)		Goddess of medicine	
Athena	Minerva	Goddess of wisdom, fertility, and war; guardian of Athens	
Cronus	Saturn	Father of Zeus; agriculture	
Dike		Justice	Acts 28:4
Demeter	Ceres	Corn-goddess; guardian of marriage	
Dionys(i)us	Bacchus (Liber)	Phrygian god; associated with nature, wine, and revelry	
Hades	Pluto (Dis)	God of the underworld	
Hephaistos (Hephaestus)	Vulcan	God of fire; patron of craftsmen	
Hera	Juno	Goddess of women	
Hermes	Mercury	God of heralds	Acts 14:12
Hestia	Vesta	Goddess of fire; cf. *vestal* virgins	
Pan	Faunus	Goat-god of shepherds	
Poseidon	Neptune	Water-god; also linked with earthquakes	
Prometheus		God of fire; created man from clay	
Tyche	Fortuna	God of destiny	
Zeus	Jupiter	Sky-god; controller of weather; ruler of all gods and men	Acts 14:12–13
	Cybele	Mother-earth	
	Emperor	Julius Caesar and Augustus Caesar were deified posthumously; Caligula, Nero, and Domitian demanded worship in their lifetime.	

Olympian gods are in bold type.

Selected Jewish and Christian Literature

Apocrypha	Letter of Jeremiah (317 B.C.)
	Tobit (250–175 B.C.)
	Baruch (200 B.C.–A.D. 70)
	Ecclesiasticus (Sirach) (190 B.C.)
	Additions of Esther (180–145 B.C.)
	Judith (175–110 B.C.)
	Song of the Three Children (167–163 B.C.)
	1 Esdras (c. 150 B.C.)
	Bel and Dragon (150–100 B.C.)
	Prayer of Manasseh (150–50 B.C.)
	Wisdom of Solomon (150 B.C.–A.D. 40)
	1 Maccabees (103–63 B.C.)
	2 Maccabees (c. 100 B.C.)
	Susanna (c. 100 B.C.?)
	2 Esdras (A.D. 70–135)
Pseudepigrapha	Enoch (200–63 B.C.)
	Letter of Aristeas (170–130 B.C.)
	Book of Jubilees (150–100 B.C.)
	Testaments of 12 Patriarchs (c. 130 B.C.)
	3 Maccabees (1st c. B.C.)
	4 Maccabees (?)
	Sibylline Oracles (c. 80 B.C.–A.D. 130)
	Psalms of Solomon (c. 40 B.C.)
	Book of Adam & Eve (1st c. A.D.)
	Lives of the Prophets (1st c. A.D.)
	Assumption of Moses (A.D. 1–30)
	2 Baruch (A.D. 70–100)
	Ascension of Isaiah (2nd c. A.D.)
Apostolic Fathers	1 Clement (A.D. 95–96)
	Ignatius (A.D. 110–117)
	The Didache (A.D. 100–130?)
	Shepherd of Hermas (A.D. 100–140)
	Epistle of Barnabas (c. A.D. 132)
	Polycarp (before 155)

Cities in the New Testament

Cities of Christ	
Bethlehem ("House of Bread")	Birthplace of the Messiah (Mic. 5:2); scene of David's anointing by Samuel; five miles south of Jerusalem; modern Beit Lahm.
Bethsaida	Rebuilt by Philip the Tetrarch, who named it Julias; modern Khirbet el-Araj.
Caesarea Philippi	Renamed by Philip the Tetrarch; originally holy place of Baal and Pan; linked by roads to Tyre and Sidon; modern Bania.
Cana	Where Jesus turned water to wine; possible site of Josephus's captivity by Roman army; modern Khirbet Qana(?).
Capernaum	Border town between tetrarchies of Herod Antipas and Herod Philip; on shore of Sea of Galilee; on main highway; occupied by military guard; mixed population; modern Tell Hum.
Chorazin	Town two miles north of Capernaum; famous for wheat; modern Kerazeh.
Decapolis ("Ten Cities")	Occupied by Greek colonists from about 200 B.C.; came under Jewish control in Maccabean times; formed into a league for mutual defense; original members (according to Pliny) were Damascus, Dion, Gadara, Gerasa, Hippos, Kanatha, Pella, Philadelphia, Raphana, Sycthopolis.
Gennesaret	Region on northwest shore of the Sea of Galilee.
Jericho	New Testament site different from original Old Testament site; located near ford of Jordan and main trade route; location of winter palace of Herods; modern Tulul Abu el-Alyiq.
Jerusalem	Taken by David the king from the Jebusites; capital of Israel and later Judea; place where Christ was crucified; center of Judaism in the first century A.D.; where temple was located; destroyed in A.D. 70 by Titus.
Nain	Where Jesus raised widow's son; southeast of Nazareth; modern Nein.
Nazareth	Boyhood home of Jesus; enclosed by hills except on south; modern en-Nasirah.
Sidon	Seaport; major city of Phoenicia, in Roman province of Syria; enjoyed a degree of self-government; celebrated for poets, philosophers, and a law school.
Sychar	City of Samaritan woman (John 4); probably modern el-Askar.
Tyre	Seaport; major city of Phoenicia, in Roman province of Syria; enjoyed right of self-government; produced Stoic philosopher Apollonius; highly-valued exports: wine and purple material.

Cities Paul Visited	
Antioch (Pisidia)	Administrative center for southern Galatia; ethnically Phrygian; major stopping point on trade route from Ephesus to the Euphrates; sanctuary to the god-men (cf. Greek Dionysius or Apollo) in nearby hills.
Antioch (Syria)	Third largest city in Roman Empire (after Rome and Alexandria); founded on Orontes River by Seleucus Nicator; capital.
Athens	For centuries the chief city of the province of Attica and the center of Greek thought. Athens is famous for the Acropolis, a flat rock plateau that rises about 200 feet above the plain around it, upon which are the remains of several masterpieces of architecture.[1] Paul gave the philosophers there the message of the gospel using their own arguments (Acts 17:15–24). For further information, see standard reference works.
Berea	On tableland of fertile farm country; modern Verria.
Caesarea	Rebuilt by Herod the Great, 25–10 B.C., named for Caesar Augustus; major Mediterranean port; large amphitheater and temple (of emperor); residence of Judean procurators; modern Qaisariyeh.
Corinth	Capital of Achaia, located on Isthmus; destroyed by Rome 146 B.C., rebuilt by Julius Caesar 44 B.C.; host of biennial Isthmian games, at site of which was stadium, theater, and temple of Poseidon; temple of Apollo stood here since sixth century B.C.; temple of Aphrodite employed 1,000 priestesses as ritual prostitutes.
Damascus	Ancient Syrian city antedating Abraham: oldest continually inhabited large city in the world; fortified city with houses on the wall; successively under control of Seleucid kings, Nabatean kings Aretas III and IV, and Rome.
Derbe	On frontier of Galatia; ethnically Lycaonian; modern Kerti Huyuk.
Ephesus	See next section: Cities of the Seven Churches of the Apocalypse.
Iconium	Ethnically Phrygian; capital of Lycaonia 63 B.C.; incorporated into Galatia 25 B.C.; located on plateau in mountainous region; modern Konya.
Lystra	Founded as Roman colony in Galatia c. 6 B.C.; ethnically Lycaonian.
Miletus	Important Greek city located at the mouth of the Meander River, near Ephesus. Paul visited there on his last missionary journey (Acts 20:15–17). From Miletus he sailed for Tyre. Paul left Trophimus in Miletus because he was ill (2 Tim. 4:20).[2]

[1] Walter A. Elwell and Barry J. Beitzel, *Baker Encyclopedia of the Bible* (Grand Rapids: Baker, 1988), 230.
[2] Ibid., 1459.

Paphos	Capital of Cyprus; rebuilt after earthquake 15 B.C.; housed shrine of Venus-Aphrodite.
Philippi	Roman colony on Via Egnatia, main Roman highway through Greece; Octavian and Antony defeated Brutus and Cassius on the Philippian plain 42 B.C.; exempted from imperial taxes.
Rome	Capital of the Roman Empire on the Tiber River in present-day Italy. Traditionally founded in 753 B.C. For centuries the most important city in the Western world. Home to Rome's emperors, senators, and military leaders as well as the center of Latin thought. Paul came to the city under imperial escort and, according to tradition, was martyred there sometime between A.D. 65 and 67.
Salamis	Main port and commercial center of Cyprus; largest agora (marketplace) in Roman colonies.
Thessalonica	Naval base and port city on Gulf of Thessalonica, in view of Mt. Olympus; capital of Macedonia; modern Salonika.
Troas	City in Turkey on the Aegean shore, 10 miles south of the ancient site of Troy. An important seaport during the time of Paul because it was the easiest and shortest route from Asia to Europe. On their second missionary journey, Paul and Silas came to Troas after being forbidden to preach the Word in Asia (Acts 16:6). Paul sailed from Troas into Macedonia (Acts 16:8–9). Later, after his mission in Ephesus was finished, Paul stayed and preached the gospel here on his way to Jerusalem for the last time (2 Cor. 2:12). The incident of the young man's fall to his death and his resurrection occurred here (Acts 20:6–12). Paul visited Troas again and left a cloak and documents; these he wanted Timothy to bring to him at his prison in Rome (2 Tim. 4:13). There was an important church here from the earliest days.[3]
Cities of the Seven Churches of the Apocalypse	
Ephesus	(Rev. 2:1–7): Ancient city; population c. 200,000–500,000; leading port of Asia Minor; on major trade route; made free city 98 B.C.; Ephesians were Roman citizens; destructive earthquake occurred A.D. 17; theater held 25,000; famed for worship of Artemis; her priestesses were cult prostitutes; also center of emperor cult-temple built for Domitian.
Smyrna	(Rev. 2:8–11): Harbor town; population c. 200,000; wealthy academic community; had "street of gold" with a temple at each end; modern Izmir.

[3] Ibid., 2107.

Pergamum	(Rev. 2:12–17): Capital of Attalid kingdom 3rd–2nd century B.C.; second largest library in Roman Empire; famous for parchment; home of the Asclepion (health resort), great altar of Zeus, and three temples to emperor.
Thyatira	(Rev. 2:18–29): City of many trade guilds; located on imperial post road; modern Akhisar.
Sardis	(Rev. 3:1–6): Wealthy fortress city set on a hill accessible to Asia Minor's most fertile river basin; destroyed by earthquake A.D. 17, rebuilt by Tiberius.
Philadelphia	(Rev. 3:7–13): Fortress city on imperial post road; educational center for Hellenism; destroyed by earthquake A.D. 17; rebuilt by Tiberius; modern Alasehir.
Laodicea	(Rev. 3:14–22): Producer of world-famous black wool; center for banking; school of medicine; underwent two earthquakes and rebuilt once and without imperial aid; modern Eski Hisar.

First-Century Emperors, Roman Prefects over Judea, and Rulers in Israel

Emperors	Prefects	Kings, Tetrarchs, Ethnarch
AUGUSTUS, 27 B.C.–A.D. 14	Coponius, A.D. 6–9	HEROD the Great, King over all Israel, 37–4 B.C. (Matt. 2:1–19; Luke 1:5)
		ARCHELAUS, Ethnarch of Judea, Samaria, and Idumea, 4 B.C.–A.D. 6 (Matt. 2:22)
TIBERIUS, A.D. 14–37	M. Ambivius, 9–12 Annius Rufus, 12–15 Valerius Gratus, 15–26 PONTIUS PILATE, 26–36 (Luke 3:1; 23:1)	HEROD PHILIP, Tetrarch of Iturea, Trachonitus, Gaulanitis, Auranitis, and Batanea, 4 B.C.–A.D. 34 (Luke 3:1) HEROD ANTIPAS, Tetrarch of Galilee and Perea, 4 B.C.–A.D. 39 (Mark 6:14–29; Luke 3:1; 13:31–35; 23:7–12)
Caligula, 37–41	Marcellus, 36–37 Marullus, 37–41	HEROD AGRIPPA I, 37–44; by A.D. 41, King over all Israel (Acts 12:1–24)
CLAUDIUS, 41–54	Cuspius Fadus, 44–46 Tiberius Alexander, 46–48 Ventidius Cumanus, 48–52 M. Antonius FELIX, 52–60 (Acts 23:26–24:27) Porcius FESTUS, 59–62 (Acts 25)	HEROD AGRIPPA II, 50–100, Tetrarch of Chalcis and northern territory (Acts 25:13–26:32)
Nero, 54–68 (Emperor at deaths of Paul and Peter) Galba, 68 Otho, 69 Vitellius, 69 Vespasian, 69–79 Titus, 79–81 Domitian, 81–96 Nerva, 96–98 Trajan, 98–117	Albinus, 62–64 Gessius Florus, 64–66 Vettulenus Cerialis, 70–72 Lucilius Bassus, 72–75 M. Salvienus, 73–81 Pompeius Longinus, 86	

Names in caps are mentioned by name in the New Testament.

Roman Emperors in the Time of the New Testament

Emperor	Dates of Reigns	Contact with the NT Account
Imperator Caesar *Augustus* (Octavian)	27 B.C.–A.D. 14	Birth of Jesus; census occurred, which caused Joseph and Mary to go to Bethlehem; the beginning of the emperor cult, against which Christians later resisted and were persecuted by Rome (Luke 2:1).
Tiberius Julius Caesar Augustus	14–37	Jesus had His public ministry and died during the reign of this emperor (Luke 3:1).
Gaius Caesar Augustus Germanicus (Caligula)	37–41	He demanded worship of himself; ordered his statue placed in the Temple of Jerusalem but died before the order was carried out.
Tiberius *Claudius* Caesar Augustus Germanicus	41–54	Expelled Jewish residents from Rome, among them Priscilla and Aquila (Acts 18:2), for disputation and disturbance over one named "Chrestus" (Acts 11:28).
Imperator *Nero* Claudius Caesar Augustus Germanicus	54–68	First real persecution of Christians by Rome, though only around the city of Rome; Peter and Paul martyred (Acts 25:10; 28:19).
Servius *Galba* Imperator Caesar Augustus	68	Siege of Jerusalem took place in the time of this emperor and the next two.
Imperator Marcus *Otho* Caesar Augustus	69	
Aulus *Vitellius* Imperator Germanicus Augustus	69	
Imperator Caesar *Vespasianus* Augustus	69–79	He was the general in charge of crushing Jerusalem rebellion in the late 60s, but upon the death of Nero he proceeded to Rome to become emperor, leaving the task to his son Titus, who besieged Jerusalem until its fall, and that of the temple, in A.D. 70.
Imperator *Titus* Caesar Vespasianus Augustus	79–81	He was the general who conquered Jerusalem against the Jewish Zealots in A.D. 70.
Imperator Caesar *Domitianus* Augustus Germanicus	81–96	Persecution of the church during his reign; he demanded to be called Lord and God (*Dominus et Deus*); his persecution probably served as the background for the writing of the Apocalypse (Revelation) to encourage Christians.

First-Century Prefects of Judea

Prefects	Dates	Contact with New Testament
Coponius	A.D. 6–9	
Ambivius	9–12	
Annius Rufus (Rifinus)	12–15	
Valerius Gratus	15–26	
Pontius Pilate	26–36	Crucifixion of Jesus under Pontius Pilate (Luke 3:1; 23:1)
Marcellus	36–37	
Marullus	37–41	
No procurator Herod Agrippa I was king over Judea and all Palestine	41–44	
Cuspius Fadus	44–46	
Tiberius Julius Alexander	46–48	
Ventidius Cumanus	48–52	
M. Antonius Felix	52–60	Paul tried before him (Acts 23–24)
Porcius Festus	60–62	Paul tried before him, and appealed to Caesar (Acts 24:27)
Albinus	62–64	
Gessius Florus	64–66	From 66–70 Jerusalem in rebellion and then under siege by Vespasian and later Titus
Vettulenus Cerialis	Destruction of Jerusalem to 72	
Lucilius Bassus	72–75	
M. Salvienus	73–81	
Pompeius Longinus	86	

The Ptolemies

Title (Appelation)	Years
Ptolemy I (Soter)	306–282 B.C.
Ptolemy II (Philadelphus)	282–246
Ptolemy III (Euergetes)	246–221
Ptolemy IV (Philopator)	221–203
Ptolemy V (Epiphanes)	203–181
Ptolemy VI (Philometor)	181–145
Ptolemy VIII[1] (Euergetes II, "Physcon")	145–116
Cleopatra III and Ptolemy IX (Soter II, "Lathyrus")	116–108
Cleopatra III and Ptolemy X (Alexander)	108–88
Ptolemy VIII (Soter II, "Lathyrus")	88–80
Ptolemy XI (Alexander II)	80
Ptolemy XII (Auletes)	80–51
Cleopatra VII	51–30

This is a general listing of the Ptolemaic (and, in the next chart, the Seleucid) succession of rulers. Because the kingdoms were wracked with political intrigue, murder, rebellion, and incest, they were never entirely united, nor was the succession of rulers as simple as the list suggests.

[1] Ptolemy VII did not physically rule.

The Seleucids

Title (Appelation)	Years
Seleucus I (Nicator)	312/11–280 B.C.
Antiochus I (Soter)	281–261
Antiochus II (Theos)	261–246
Seleucus II (Callinicus)	247–225
Seleucus III	225–223
Antiochus III (The Great)	223–187
Seleucus IV (Philopator)	187–175
Antiochus IV (Epiphanes)	175–163
Antiochus V (Eupator)	163–162
Demetrius I (Soter)	162–150
Alexander Balas	150–145
Demetrius II (Nicator)	145-139
Antiochus VI (Epiphanes)	145–142
Antiochus VII (Sidetes)	139–129
Demetrius II (Nicator)	129–125
Antiochus VIII (Grypus)	125–96
Antiochus IX (Chzicenus)	113–95
Antiochus X (Eusobes)	94–92 or 83
Antiochus XIII (Asiaticus)	83–64

The Maccabees

Name	Years
Mattathias	168–166 B.C.
Judas Maccabeus	166–160
Jonathan Maccabeus	160–143
Simon Maccabeus	143–135
John Hyrcanus	135–104
Aristobulus	104–103
Alexander Jannaeus	103–76
Alexandra Salome	76–67
Hyrcanus II vs. Aristobulus II	67–63
Hyrcanus II	63–40
Antigonus	40–37

The Jewish High Priests

Name	Years
Jaddua	c. 350–320 B.C.
Onias I	c. 320–290
Simon I	c. 290–275
Eleazar	c. 275–260
Manasseh	c. 260–245
Onias II	c. 245–220
Simon II (The Righteous)	c. 220–198
Onias III	c. 198–174
*Jason	174–171
*Menelaus	171–162
*Alcimius	162–159
No high priest in Jerusalem	159–152
*JONATHAN†	152–143
SIMON	*143–135
JOHN HYRCANUS	135–104
ARISTOBULUS I	104–103
ALEXANDER JANNAEUS	103–76
HYRCANUS II	76–67
ARISTOBULUS II	67–63
*HYRCANUS II	63–40
ANTIGONUS	40–37
*Hananel	37–36
*ARISTOBULUS III	36
*Hananel	36–30
*Jeshua, son of Phabes	30–23

*Appointed by a gentile leader.

†Names in capitals indicate Hasmoneans.

A variation of a year in either direction is possible.

The Jewish High Priests *Continued*

Name	Years
*Simon, son of Boethus	23–05
*Matthais, son of Theophilus	c. 5
*Joseph, son of Ellem	c. 5–4
*Joazar, son of Boethus	c. 4
*Eleazar, son of Boethus	c. 4–3
*Jeshua, son of See	3 B.C.–A.D. 6
*Joazar, son of Boethus	6
*Annas, son of Seth	6–15
*Ishmael, son of Phiabi I	15–16
*Eleazar, son of Annas	16–17
*Simon, son of Camithus	17–18
*Joseph Caiaphas	18–36
Jonathan, son of Annas	36–37
*Theophilus, son of Annas	37–41
*Simon Kantheras, son of Boethus	41–42
*Matthias, son of Annas	42–43
*Elioenai, son of Kantheras	43–44
*Joseph, son of Camei/Cambyus	c. 44–47
*Ananias, son of Nebedaius	c. 47–59
*Ishmael, son of Phiabi II	c. 59–61
*Joseph of Cabi	61–62
*Ananus, son of Ananus	62
*Jesus, son of Damnaeus	c. 62–63
*Jeshua, son of Gamaliel	c. 63–65
*Matthias, son of Theophilus	65–67
Phinehas of Habta	67–70

*Appointed by a gentile leader.

†Names in capitals indicate Hasmoneans.

A variation of a year in either direction is possible.

A Genealogical Chart of the Herodian Dynasty

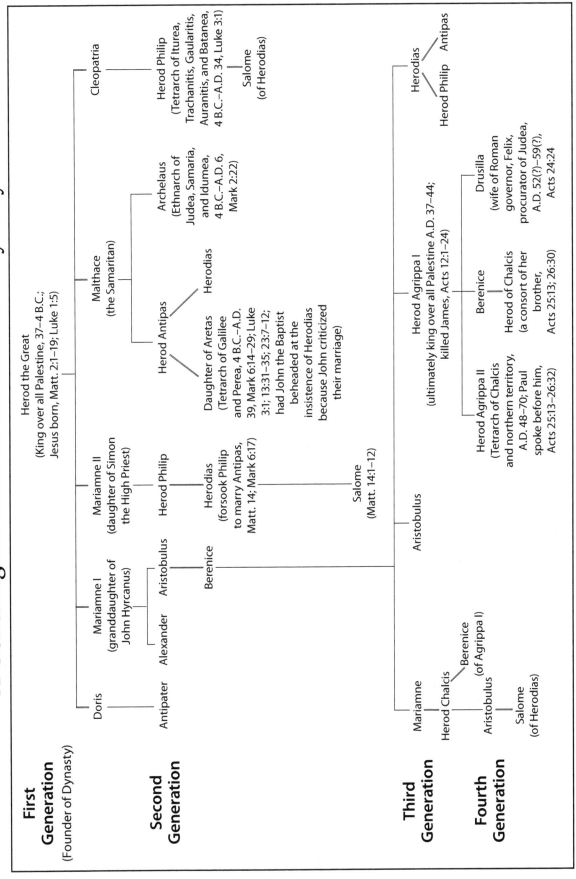

Reigning kings of New Testament times are in red. This is only a partial genealogy.

First Generation
(Founder of Dynasty)

Herod the Great
(King over all Palestine, 37–4 B.C.;
Jesus born, Matt. 2:1–19; Luke 1:5)

Doris — Mariamne I (granddaughter of John Hyrcanus) — Mariamne II (daughter of Simon the High Priest) — Malthace (the Samaritan) — Cleopatria

Second Generation

Antipater

Alexander   Aristobulus

Herod Philip

Herod Antipas
(Tetrarch of Galilee and Perea, 4 B.C.–A.D. 39, Mark 6:14–29; Luke 3:1; 13:31–35; 23:7–12; had John the Baptist beheaded at the insistence of Herodias because John criticized their marriage)

Archelaus
(Ethnarch of Judea, Samaria, and Idumea, 4 B.C.–A.D. 6, Mark 2:22)

Herod Philip
(Tetrarch of Iturea, Trachanitis, Gaularitis, Auranitis, and Batanea, 4 B.C.–A.D. 34, Luke 3:1)

Berenice

Herodias
(forsook Philip to marry Antipas, Matt. 14; Mark 6:17)

Daughter of Aretas

Herodias

Salome
(of Herodias)

Salome
(Matt. 14:1–12)

Third Generation

Mariamne

Herod Chalcis

Aristobulus

Herod Agrippa I
(ultimately king over all Palestine A.D. 37–44; killed James, Acts 12:1–24)

Herodias   Herod Philip   Antipas

Fourth Generation

Berenice
(of Agrippa I)

Aristobulus

Salome
(of Herodias)

Herod Agrippa II
(Tetrarch of Chalcis and northern territory, A.D. 48–70; Paul spoke before him, Acts 25:13–26:32)

Berenice

Herod of Chalcis
(a consort of her brother, Acts 25:13; 26:30)

Drusilla
(wife of Roman governor, Felix, procurator of Judea, A.D. 52(?)–59(?), Acts 24:24)

Jewish Sects of the First Century

Sects	Origin	Historical Background	Theology	Contact with NT	Demise
Hassideans (Ḥassidim)	Name means "pious ones." They were concerned primarily with religious reform, organized during the 4th and 3rd centuries B.C.	The Ḥassideans formed the nucleus of the Maccabean revolt and resisted any Hellenization under the Syrians. They have been linked with the Essenes because of their careful religious observance, but most likely they are the spiritual forebears of the Pharisees.	1 Macc. 2:42 says they "were mighty men in Israel . . . such as were devoted to the law." The Talmud refers to them. They strictly obeyed the commandments, had fervent prayers, and rigidly observed the Sabbath.	None	Probably found in the Pharisees
Pharisees	Surfaced as a religious and political party during the second-temple period (516 B.C.–A.D. 70) briefly after the Maccabean revolt about 165–160 B.C. They probably came from the Ḥassidim. *Pharisee* may be from Hebrew stem that means "to be separated"; they separated from pagan practices and forces.	Arising from the mass of people, the Pharisees waged a vigorous struggle to remove Jewish religion from the control of the priests. They removed several ceremonies from the temple and placed them in the Jewish home. While the Sadducees occupied themselves with the temple, the Pharisees proclaimed to the people the law of God. They were more liberal and flexible in interpreting the law of God than were the Sadducees.	God is omnipotent, all-wise, all-knowing, and all-present; God has created in man two impulses, one to do evil and the other good, urging him to do good; man has the free will to choose. The Torah consists of Written Law and Oral Law, both revealed by God to Moses; the Torah was to be interpreted with God-given reason, in view of the ideas of the knowledge of each age; not sacrifice but study of Torah was true worship; God is in total control, helping people to do good, and permitting them to do evil; believed in life after death, resurrection, and angels and other spirits.	Probably NT references against the Pharisees were against the insincere ones, who were even condemned by their fellows (cf. Sotah III:4 and 22b). These Pharisees are called hypocrites and vipers (Matt. 23:5, 23ff.; Luke 18:1ff.); Nicodemus and Joseph of Arimathea were both Pharisees (cf. John 3 and Mark 15:43); Paul was proud of his heritage as a Pharisee (Acts 22). Pharisaic beliefs were in keeping with much of early Christian theology.	After the destruction of the temple in A.D. 70, the Pharisees continued to rule over a reconstituted Sanhedrin. In A.D. 135, after another Jewish revolt, the Sanhedrin was dispersed. However, Pharisaic teaching became the basis for rabbinic teaching, which continues to this day.

Sects	Origin	Historical Background	Theology	Contact with NT	Demise
Sadducees	Name may have developed from Zadok, the high priest in the days of David (2 Sam. 8:17; 15:24) and Solomon (1 Kings 1:34–35; 1 Chron. 12:28). Ezek. 40:46; 43:19; 44:10–15 shows this family worthy to control the temple. A Sadducee, then, may be one who is a sympathizer of the Zadokites; formed about 200 B.C. as the party of the high priests and aristocratic families; not all priests were Sadducees.	They controlled the temple and the affairs of the country, as representatives of the priestly aristocracy, supporting the Hasmonean rulers. Even under Roman rule, through the Sanhedrin rule, in which many were members, they exercised considerable political control over the people of Palestine; they were more apt to adopt Hellenism and were in favor with Roman authorities.	They had a more anthropomorphic view of God than did the Pharisees; as the conservative element in Jewish religion, they rejected the Oral Law, and accepted only the Written Law of Moses; they denied the resurrection of the body and the existence of angels; emphasized the sacrificial cult of the temple; considered God not to be interested in human affairs, and so rejected divine providence.	Since they were the political group and were considerably opposed to Christian doctrine (Matt. 22:23; Mark 12:18; Acts 4:5; 23:8), the church had most to fear from the Sadducees.	A.D. 70, with the destruction of the temple
Zealots	Some think they were active as early as 37 B.C., while others say around A.D. 66. Although they are not mentioned by name until A.D. 66, Judas of Galilee is thought to be a key precursor of the Zealots. Around A.D. 6 he led a revolt against Roman taxation that was crushed violently. However, his sons continued in his place, eventually being executed by Tiberias Julias Alexander in A.D. 46.	They were extremely opposed to Roman rule over Palestine and would not tolerate peace with idolatrous Rome; their religious zeal gave them their name; they refused to pay taxes and terrorized their political opponents and Roman rulers.	They were fanatics for the Jewish faith and Torah.	Zealots are mentioned in Luke 6:15; the term is used as a designation of Simon (Luke 6:15; Acts 1:13). *Cananaean* is from a Hebrew word meaning "to be zealous" (Matt. 10:4; Mark 3:18, NRSV).	A.D. 73

Sects	Origin	Historical Background	Theology	Contact with NT	Demise
Sicarii	This was an extreme Zealot group that arose to oppose Roman rule; their name comes from the Greek word for "daggerman," who would stab those friendly to Rome when intended victims were in large crowds.	In A.D. 50–70 bands of assassins plundered and terrorized Judea. They were in charge of the revolt that brought the destruction of Jerusalem; many fled to Masada.	They were the same as the Zealots in theology.	They are mentioned in Acts 21:38 as "terrorists."	A.D. 73
Essenes	Started in Maccabean times, latter half of second-temple period (c. second century B.C.–A.D. 70); origination of name is uncertain.	About four thousand were scattered in the villages and towns of Judea; some lived at Qumran, the location of the Dead Sea Scrolls. They developed possibly in reaction to low repute of the priesthood of the Sadducees; they have been identified with the Hassidim, Zealots, and even with Greek or Iranian elements.	They were most strict, refrained from marriage; ascetics; believed in communal property; they considered themselves the recipients of the promises to Israel through the prophets; rejected temple worship as polluted; they had more rigid Sabbath-law requirements than did the Pharisees; they had strict observance of ceremonial washings, daily prayers, and continuous study of Old Testament; very apocalyptically oriented.	Possibly John the Baptist came into contact with them.	uncertain

Christ and Christianity in Jewish and Pagan Sources

Name	Source	Date	Statement	Comment
Flavius Josephus	*Jewish Antiquities* 18.63–64	A.D. 93–94	About this time arose Jesus, a wise man (if indeed it be right to call him a man). For he was a doer of marvelous deeds, and a teacher of men who gladly receive the truth. He drew to himself many persons, both of the Jews and also of the Gentiles. (He was the Christ.) And when Pilate, upon the indictment of the leading men among us, had condemned him to the cross, those who had loved him at the first did not cease to do so (for he appeared to them alive on the third day—the godly prophets having foretold these and ten thousand other things about him). And even to this day the race of Christians, who are named from him, has not died out.	When Pilate and the Jews were at odds over the use of the temple funds by him to build an aqueduct in Jerusalem. The parenthetical statements are highly suspect as having come from Josephus. Most likely they were added by a Christian scribe (only Christians transmitted Josephus, since the Jews rejected him as a traitor to Judaism) before the time of Eusebius's *Ecclesiastical History* (A.D. 325). Also, there may have been deletions. Cf. F. F. Bruce, *Jesus and Christian Origins outside the New Testament*, 39ff.
	Jewish Antiquities 20.200	93–94	… he (Annas the younger) convened a judicial session of the Sanhedrin and brought before it the brother of Jesus the so-called Christ—James by name—and some others, whom he charged with breaking the law and handed over to be stoned to death.	Appears to be an unaltered and genuine statement.
Babylonian Talmud	*Sanhedrin* 43a	source from 70–200, later compiled in Talmud	Jesus was hanged on Passover Eve. Forty days previously the herald had cried, "He is being led out for stoning, because he practiced sorcery and led Israel astray and enticed them into apostasy. Whosoever has anything to say in his defence, let him come and declare it." As nothing was brought forward in his defence, he was hanged on Passover Eve.	It is significant that the charge against Jesus was concerning the religious law of Israel rather than Roman law.

Name	Source	Date	Statement	Comment
	Sanhedrin 43a (appended remarks)	ibid.	(Rabbi) Ulla said, "Would you believe that any defence would have been so zealously sought for him? He was a deceiver, and the All-merciful says: 'You shall not spare him, neither shall you conceal him.' It was different with Jesus, for he was near to the kingship."	A Jewish apologetic note against Christians may be present here. "Near to the kingship" is a reference to His descent from David.
Babylonian Talmud	*Sanhedrin* 43a	ibid.	The rabbis taught: Jesus had five disciples: Mathai, Naqai, Nezer, Buni, and Todah.	This has little historical value. Mathai may be Matthew; Todah perhaps is Thaddaeus; Naqai conceivably is Nicodemus; Buni may be a form of Boanerges; and Nezer may relate to Nazarene.
Pliny (the Younger)	*Epistles* 10.96 "Letter to Trajan"	c. 110	(Christians) . . . maintained . . . that their fault or error amounted to nothing more than this: they were in the habit of meeting on a certain fixed day before sunrise and reciting an antiphonal hymn to Christ as God, and binding themselves with an oath—not to commit any crime, but to abstain from all acts of theft, robbery and adultery, from breaches of faith, from repudiating a trust when called upon to honor it. After this . . . it was their custom to separate, and then to meet again to partake of food. . . .	The letter is too lengthy to produce in full. Pliny as legate of Bithynia wrote Trajan concerning how to deal with the rapid growth of Christians in his area.
Tacitus	*Annals* 15.44	between 115 and 117	But all human effort, all the lavish gifts of the emperor, and the propitiations of the gods, did not banish the sinister belief that the conflagration was the result of an order. Consequently, to get rid of the report, Nero fastened the guilt and inflicted the most exquisite tortures on a class hated for their abominations, called Christians by the populace. Christus, from whom the name had its origin, suffered the extreme penalty during the reign of Tiberius at the hand of one of our procurators, Pontius Pilate, and a deadly superstition, thus checked for the moment, again broke out not only in Judaea, the first source of the evil, but also in the City, where all things hideous and shameful from every part of the world meet and become popular.	

Name	Source	Date	Statement	Comment
Mara bar Serapion	Syriac MS in British Museum. Additional 14.658	sometime after 73, probably in 2nd or 3rd centuries	What advantage did the Athenians gain from putting Socrates to death? Famine and plague came upon them as a judgment for their crime. What advantage did the men of Samos gain from burning Pythagoras? In a moment their land was covered with sand. What advantage did the Jews gain from executing their wise King? It was just after that that their kingdom was abolished. God justly avenged these three wise men: the Athenians died of hunger; the Samians were overwhelmed by the sea; the Jews, ruined and driven from their land, live in complete dispersion. But Socrates did not die for good; he lived on in the teaching of Plato. Pythagoras did not die for good; he lived on in the statue of Hera. Nor did the wise King die for good; he lived on in the teaching which he had given.	The writer was probably not a Christian or he would have said that Jesus rose from the dead. He simply places Jesus on a par with other wise men of antiquity. He was most likely influenced by Christians, since he blames the Jews rather than the Romans for the execution of Jesus.
Suetonius	*Life of Claudius* 25.4	120	He expelled the Jews from Rome, on account of the riots in which they were constantly indulging, at the instigation of Chrestus.	*Chrestus* was a popular misspelling of the Greek *Christos*. Suetonius apparently misunderstood the police records, thinking that Chrestus was in Rome and a ringleader of the riots in A.D. 49.
	Life of Nero 16.2	120	Punishment was inflicted on the Christians, a body of people addicted to a novel and mischievous superstition.	This statement refers to the persecution by Nero c. A.D. 64.

The base for this chart is primarily from F. F. Bruce, *Jesus and Christian Origins outside the New Testament* (Grand Rapids: Eerdmans, 1974); Bruce M. Metzger, *The New Testament: Its Background, Growth and Content* (New York: Abingdon, 1965).

Jewish Sacred and Civil Year

Numbers	Names of Months		Farm Seasons	Special Days	Scriptural Reference
1 (7)	Nisan	(Mar–Apr)	Barley harvest begins	14—Passover 15—Unleavened Bread 21—Close of Passover Commemoration of the Exodus from Egypt; marked the beginning ("firstfruits") of barley harvest.	Exod. 12:1–20; Lev. 23:5; Lev. 23:6–8
2 (8)	Iyar	(Apr–May)	Barley harvest		
3 (9)	Sivan	(May–June)	Wheat harvest	6—Feast of Pentecost—seven weeks from Passover (the anniversary of the giving of the law on Mt. Sinai). Marked the end of the harvest.	Lev. 23:15–21
4 (10)	Tammuz	(June–July)			
5 (11)	Ab	(July–Aug)	Grape, fig, olive ripe		
6 (12)	Elul	(Aug–Sept)	Vintage begins		
7 (1)	Tishri	(Sept–Oct)	Early rains; plowing	1 & 2—Feast of Trumpets—*Rosh Hashanah*—(beginning of civil year); end of grape and olive harvests.	Lev. 23:23–35
				10—Day of Atonement (*Yom Kippur*)—day of national repentance, fasting and atonement; not called "a feast."	Lev. 23:26–32
				15–22—Feast of Tabernacles—Commemoration of the living in tents on the way from Egypt to Canaan—joyous feast during which time people lived in temporary tents made of branches.	Lev. 23:33–44

Numbers	Names of Months		Farm Seasons	Special Days	Scriptural Reference
8 (2)	Heshvan	(Oct–Nov)	Wheat, barley sown		
9 (3)	Kislev	(Nov–Dec)		25—Feast of Lights, or Dedication (*Hanukkah*) Commemoration of the rededication of the temple by Judas Maccabeus (164 B.C.); brilliant lights in temple area and in Jewish homes.	John 10:22
10 (4)	Tebeth	(Dec–Jan)	Rainy winter months		
11 (5)	Shebat	(Jan–Feb)	New Year for trees		
12 (6)	Adar	(Feb–Mar)	Almonds blooming	14—Feast of Purim—Commemoration of the deliverance of Israel in the time of Esther; public reading of the book of Esther in the synagogues.	Esther 9:26–28; John 5:1
13	Adar Sheni		(Intercalary month)		

Civil year, for secular affairs and for foreign kings, is included in parentheses. Also the intercalary year is included to give notice that an extra month was sometimes added to the calendar to equate the lunar year with the solar year.

The Reckoning of Passover

Galilean Method Synoptic Reckoning used by Jesus, His disciples, and Pharisees	Judean Method John's Reckoning used by Sadducees
Thursday	
Midnight	
Sunrise	
Nisan 14 3–5 p.m. Slaying of Passover lamb	
Sunset	
Last Supper Jesus arrested	Nisan 14
Friday	
Midnight	
Sunrise	
Nisan 15 6 a.m. Jesus before Pilate 9 a.m. Crucifixion 12–3 p.m. Darkness 3 p.m. Death of Jesus Burial of Jesus	3–5 p.m. Slaying of Passover lamb
Sunset	
	Nisan 15
Saturday	
Midnight	

This presentation is a matter of debate. Annie Jaubert, for example, has offered a Tuesday Passover for Jesus and his disciples and a Friday crucifixion on the official Passover, in agreement with the Book of Jubilees, in which the Passover was always celebrated on Tuesday.

Adapted by permission from Harold W. Hoehner, *Chronological Aspects of the Life of Christ* (Grand Rapids: Zondervan, 1978).

The Reckoning of Passover
(Blomberg's Proposal)

Synoptics	John
Thursday	
Sunset	
Passover Meal (Matt. 26:17, 19; Mark 14:12, 14, 16; Luke 22:7–8) Jesus seized in the garden and led to High Priest (Matt. 26:57; Mark 14:51–53; Luke 22:54)	Passover Meal (13:1ff.) Disciples think Judas leaves to buy for the rest of the Passover week (13:29) Jesus seized in the Garden and led to High Priest (18:12–13)
Friday	
Midnight	
Trial before Caiaphas (Matt. 26:57–27:1; Mark 14:53–15:1; Luke 22:54–71)	Examination by Annas (18:12–14, 19–23) Trial before Caiaphas (18:24–28)
Sunrise[1]	
Jesus before Pilate (1) (Matt. 27:11–14; Mark 15:1–5; Luke 23:1–6) Jesus before Herod (Luke 23:7–11) Jesus before Pilate (2) (Matt. 27:15–31; Mark 15:6–15; Luke 23:13–25) Crucifixion and Burial	Jewish leaders avoid defilement for afternoon meal (*chagigah*) (18:28)[2] Jesus before Pilate (18:28–19:16) Crucifixion and Burial
Sunset	
Saturday	
Midnight	

[1] According to Blomberg, "Day of the Preparation" was the standard Jewish name for Friday in Greek. "Day of the Preparation for the Passover" (John 19:14, 31), then, is simply a shorthand reference to the Friday of Passover week. Support for this interpretation is found also in Mark 15:42. See Craig Blomberg, *The Historical Reliability of the Gospels* (Downers Grove, Ill.: InterVarsity, 1987), 177–78.

[2] Blomberg suggests that the defilement in question was not for the Passover meal (therefore making Passover on Friday) but for the lunchtime meal known as the *chagigah*, which was celebrated on the first day after the first evening of Passover. He argues that defilement incurred during the morning would have been removed by sunset, a new day. See Blomberg, 177.

The Dead Sea Scrolls

	Title	Location Discovered or Designation	Comments
Biblical Texts	Isaiah*	1QIsa^a† 1QIsa^b	Complete text of Isaiah Partial scroll containing chapters 10, 13, 16, 19–30, 35–66
	Psalms	11QPs	An almost complete scroll
Deuterocanonical Texts	Tobit‡	4QTobit	Three MSS in 4Q: one Hebrew and two Aramaic
	Judith	not identified	
	Wisdom of Solomon	Khirbet Mird	Fragments in Greek
	Ecclesiasticus	2QEcclesiasticus	
	Baruch	not identified	
	1 and 2 Maccabees	not identified	
Apocrypha and Pseudepigrapha	Enoch■	1Q; 4Q 4QEnoch	Fragments discovered in 1Q. Ten MSS, all in Aramaic, found in 4Q
	Jubilees	4Q; 2Q; 1Q 4QJub	Five MSS in 4Q; two from 2Q and 1Q, respectively. Also known as "Little Genesis"
	Book of Noah	1Q	Book mentioned in Jub. 10:13; 21:10 and the Aramaic Testament of Levi
	Testament of Levi	4QTLev; 1Q	
	Testament of Naphtali	4Q(?)	
	Sayings of Moses	1QDibMos; 1Q22	Also known as "Little Deuteronomy"
	Genesis Apocryphon°	1QapGen	Originally called the Lamech Scroll (1QLamech) or Scroll of the Patriarchs
	Prayer of Nabonidus	4QNab	
Commentaries	Habakkuk	1QpHab•	The largest and most complete commentary
	Genesis		
	Second Book of Samuel	4QPs^a 4QPs^b	
	Isaiah	4QpIsa	
	Hosea	4QpHos	
	Micah	1QpMic	
	Nahum	4QpNah	
	Zephaniah	1QpZeph (1Q15)	

	Title	Location Discovered or Designation	Comments
Sectarian	Thanksgiving Hymns	1QH	
	Manual of Discipline	1QS	1QS shares many affinities with CD; cf. CD 10:6; 13:2 with 1QS 1:6 and CD 7:6 and 1QS 1:16
	War Scroll	1QM	
	Rule of Congregation	1QSª; 1Q28³	
	Benedictions	1QSᵇ; 1Q28⁶	
	Damascus Document	CD; 4QDᵇ; 6QD	Also known as Zadokite Fragments
	Book of Mysteries	1QMyst; 1Q27	
	Prayer for the Feast of Weeks	1Q34	
	The Halakhic Letter	4QMMT	
	Melchezedek	11Q	Some see parallels to the NT book of Hebrews in this fragment.
Collections	Testamonia	4QTest	A collection of passages relating to the Messiah (Deut. 18:18ff.; 5:28; Num. 24:15–17; Deut. 33:8–11)
	Florilegium	4QFlor	Portrays a Davidic Messiah and an interpreter of the Law
	Patriarchal Blessings Ordinances	4QPatrBless	

The preceding represents only a partial listing of the scrolls and fragments that have been found; it is estimated that over forty thousand fragments have been found. Also the Greek and Syro-Palestinian fragments of the New Testament found at Khirbet Mird have not been listed.

* Parts of all the Old Testament have been discovered, with the exception of Esther. The three favorite books are Isaiah, Psalms, and Deuteronomy, which, interestingly, are the most cited books of the Old Testament by New Testament authors.

† The first numeral refers to the cave in which the scroll or fragment is found; the *Q* stands for Qumran; the following letters(s) designates the Hebrew of the scroll, or the book of the Old Testament or the name of the respective book.

‡ Deuterocanonical books are those that are accepted by the Roman Catholic Church in addition to the thirty-nine books accepted by Protestants and Jews. Some of these are classified along with apocryphal books by many scholars but will be listed separately here.

▪ Apocryphal books are those that were written after the closing of the Old Testament canon and before the time of Christ. The Pseudepigrapha are books that purport to have been written by biblical characters (e.g., Enoch) but in reality were written by persons who lived much later.

° The particular scrolls and fragments given in this listing may fit classifications other than the ones to which they are assigned. Here, for example, the *Genesis Apocryphon* is classified as a Sectarian work by some authors. Many of the Commentaries also share a sectarian flavor rather than being strict biblical commentaries of events in the biblical history.

• The small *p* stands for *pesher*, a Hebrew word for a method of Jewish interpretation of the Old Testament.

Rabbinic Writings

Writings	Divisions	Dates	Contributors	Contents	Comments
Mishnah	Seeds Festivals Women Damages Holy Things Purifications	50 B.C.–A.D. 200	Tannaim	Curriculum for the study of Jewish law	The Mishnah was the basic document of Rabbinic Judaism and considered *Oral Torah*. The Mishnah was divided into six sections: *Seeds*, concerning ritual laws dealing with cultivation of the soil; *Festivals*, concerning rules and regulations on the Sabbath and holy days; *Women*, on marriage, divorce, and other family issues; *Damages*, mainly regarding compensation on damages; *Holy Things*, rules and laws on sacrifices, and other issues pertaining to the ancient temple and its ritual; *Purifications*, pertaining to the subject of cleanness and purity.
Tosefta		A.D. 100–300	Tannaim	Teachings not found in the Mishnah	Earliest commentary on the Mishnah
Palestinian Talmud	Mishnah Gemara	A.D. 300	Amoraim	Commentary on the Mishnah	Over ninety percent of the Palestinian Talmud focuses on the Mishnah.
Babylonian Talmud	Mishnah Gemara	A.D. 200 A.D. 200–500	Tannaim Amoraim	Legal portions commenting on Torah Commentary on the Mishnah	The Babylonian Talmud contains more material that is unrelated to Mishnah than does the Palestinian Talmud. Also, the Babylonian Talmud includes many more scriptural units than the Palestinian Talmud.
Midrash	Halakah Haggadah	100 B.C.–early Middle Ages	Tannaim and Amoraim	Legal sections commenting only on Torah Narratives and sermons on any part of Old Testament	Halakah is the legal part of the Midrash, usually derived from OT. Haggadah embraces nonlegal interests infrequently encountered in the Mishnah.

PART III
The Gospels

Literary Relationships of the Synoptic Gospels

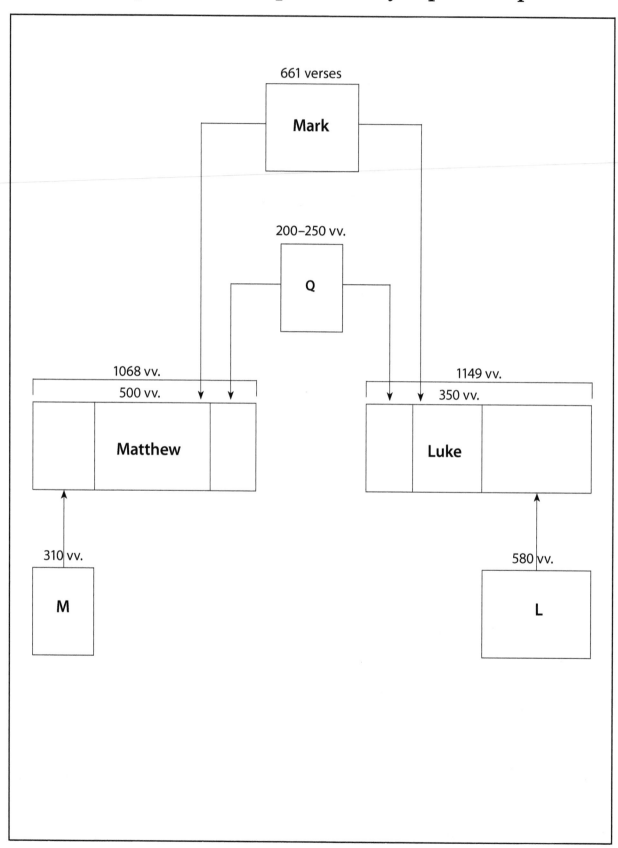

Suggested Solutions to the Synoptic Problem

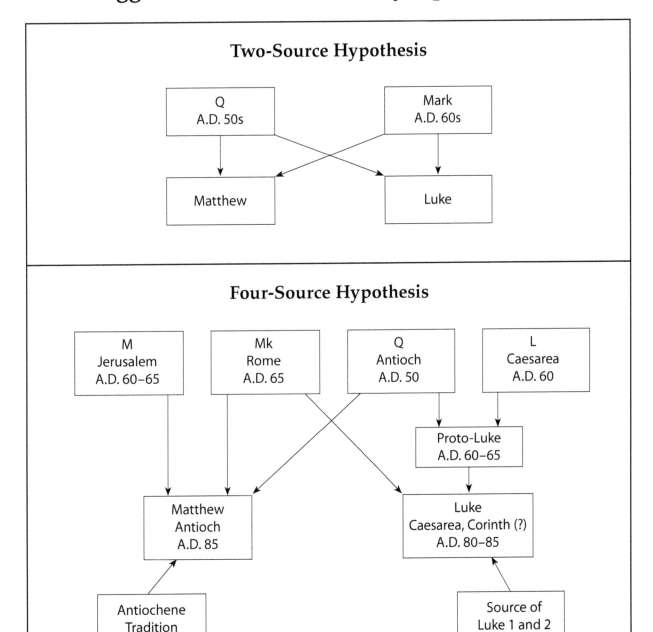

Two-Source Hypothesis

Q
A.D. 50s

Mark
A.D. 60s

Matthew

Luke

Four-Source Hypothesis

M
Jerusalem
A.D. 60–65

Mk
Rome
A.D. 65

Q
Antioch
A.D. 50

L
Caesarea
A.D. 60

Proto-Luke
A.D. 60–65

Matthew
Antioch
A.D. 85

Luke
Caesarea, Corinth (?)
A.D. 80–85

Antiochene
Tradition

Source of
Luke 1 and 2

The above schema have several undemonstrable hypotheses as to the nature, existence, locations, and dates of the proposed sources. The borrowing of Matthew and Luke from Mark appears probable. That Matthew and Luke also borrowed from an oral or written source (Q) appears reasonable. That Matthew and Luke also borrowed from sources peculiar to themselves is probable. Whether these sources were written, oral, or a combination is uncertain. And exactly which passages in Matthew and Luke are representative of specific sources is debated.

Contents of Hypothetical Q

I. The Preparation
A. John's preaching of repentance (Luke 3:7–9; Matt. 3:7–10)
B. The temptation of Jesus (Luke 4:1–13; Matt. 4:1–11)

II. Sayings
A. Beatitudes (Luke 6:20–23; Matt. 5:3–4, 6, 11–12)
B. Love to one's enemies (Luke 6:27–36; Matt. 5:39–42, 44–48; 7:12)
C. Judging (Luke 6:37–42; Matt. 7:1–5; 10:24; 15:14)
D. Hearers and doers of the Word (Luke 6:47–49; Matt. 7:24–27)

III. Narrative
A. The centurion's servant (Luke 7:1–10; Matt. 7:28a; 8:5–10, 13)
B. The Baptist's question (Luke 7:18–20; Matt. 11:2–3)
C. Christ's answer (Luke 7:22–35; Matt. 11:4–19)

IV. Discipleship
A. On the cost of discipleship (Luke 9:57–60; Matt. 8:19–22)
B. The mission charge (Luke 10:2–16; Matt. 9:37–38; 10:9–15; 11:21–23)
C. Christ's thanksgiving to the Father (Luke 10:21–24; Matt. 11:25–27; 13:16–17)

V. Various Sayings
A. The pattern prayer (Luke 11:2–4; Matt. 6:9–13)
B. An answer to prayer (Luke 11:9–13; Matt. 7:7–11)
C. The Beelzebub discussion and its sequel (Luke 11:14–23; Matt. 12:22–30)
D. Sign of the prophet Jonah (Luke 11:29–32; Matt. 12:38–42)
E. About light (Luke 11:33–36; Matt. 5:15; 6:22–23)

VI. Discourse against the Pharisees
(Luke 11:37–12:1; Matt. 23)

VII. Sayings
A. About fearless confession (Luke 12:2–12; Matt. 10:19, 26–33; 12:32)
B. On cares about earthly things (Luke 12:22–34; Matt. 6:19–21, 25–33)
C. On faithfulness (Luke 12:39–46; Matt. 24:43–51)
D. On signs for this age (Luke 12:51–56; Matt. 10:34–36; 16:2–3)
E. On agreeing with one's adversaries (Luke 12:57–59; Matt. 5:25–26)

VIII. Parables of the Mustard Seed and Leaven
(Luke 13:18–21; Matt. 13:31–33)

IX. Other Sayings
A. Condemnation of Israel (Luke 13:23–30; Matt. 7:13–14, 22–23; 8:11–12)
B. Lament over Jerusalem (Luke 13:34–35; Matt. 23:37–39)
C. Cost of discipleship (Luke 14:26–35; Matt. 10:37–38; 5:13)
D. On serving two masters (Luke 16:13; Matt. 6:24)
E. On law and divorce (Luke 16:16–18; Matt. 11:12–13; 5:18, 32)
F. On offenses, forgiveness, and faith (Luke 17:1–6; Matt. 18:6–7, 15, 20–22)
G. The day of the Son of Man (Luke 17:23–27, 33–37; Matt. 24:17–18, 26–28, 37–41)

Scholars disagree as to the contents of Q.

Adapted from Ralph Martin, *The Four Gospels.* New Testament Foundations: A Guide for Christian Students, rev. ed., vol. 1 (Eugene, Ore.: Wipf & Stock, 2000).

Material Unique to Matthew

Annunciation to Joseph of birth			1:18–25
The wise men			2:1–12
Flight to Egypt and return			2:13–23
Instructions in Sermon on the Mount:			
On the Law	5:17–20	On fasting	6:16–18
On murder	5:21–26	On trusting the Father	6:19–34
On oaths	5:33–37	On prayer	7:7–11
On nonresistance	5:38–42	On entrance by the narrow	7:13–14
On almsgiving	6:1–4	gate	

Jesus speaking with authority	7:28–29
Healing of blind and dumb	9:27–34
The harvest is great	9:35–38
The way of a disciple	10:16–42
Condemnation of the cities	11:20–24
Call to discipleship	11:25–30

Parables

Tares	13:24–30, 36–43	Dragnet	13:47–50
Hidden treasure	13:44	Treasures new and old	13:51–52
Pearl of great value	13:45–46		

Peter … the rock	16:17–19
Payment of temple tax	17:24–27
Forgiveness	18:15–22
Parable of unforgiving servant	18:23–35
Parable of vineyard workers	20:1–16
Parable of two sons	21:28–32
Denunciation of external spirituality	23:8–12
Condemnation of scribes and Pharisees	23:13–39
End times	24:32–41
Admonition on readiness	24:42–44
Parable of the wise and wicked servants	24:45–51
Parable of ten virgins	25:1–13
Sheep and goats	25:31–46
Death of Judas	27:3–10
The guard at the tomb	27:62–66
Report of the guard	28:11–15
The Great Commission	28:16–20

Much of the above is assigned to the hypothetical source M.

Material Unique to Mark

Parable of automatic growth	4:26–29
Deaf and dumb man healed	7:31–37
Blind man healed at Bethsaida	8:22–26
Forgiveness conditioned on our forgiving	11:25–26
A young man who fled	14:51–52
The Great Commission[1]	16:14–18

[1] Most scholars think Mark 16:9–20 was not part of Mark's original Gospel.

Material Unique to Luke

Dedication to Theophilus	1:1–4
Gabriel and Zechariah	1:5–25
Gabriel and Mary	1:26–38
Mary and Elizabeth	1:39–45
Birth of John the Baptist	1:57–66
Zechariah's prophecy	1:67–80
Census, journey to Bethlehem, full inn	2:1–7
Angels and shepherds	2:8–20
Circumcision and temple offering	2:21–40
Boy Jesus in the temple	2:41–52
Date of John the Baptist	3:1–2
Specific teachings of John	3:10–14
The Lucan genealogy	3:23–37
Jesus rejected at Nazareth	4:16–21
Large catch of fish; calling of Simon	5:5–11
Widow's son at Nain	7:11–17
Sinful woman forgiven	7:36–50
Women who supported Jesus	8:1–3
Rejection by Samaritan village	9:51–56
The seventy-two sent out*	10:1–12
The seventy-two return*	10:17–20
The Good Samaritan	10:29–37
Mary and Martha	10:38–42
The importunate friend	11:9–13a
True blessedness	11:27–28
Parable of the rich fool	12:13–21
Much given, much demanded	12:41–50
Repent or perish	13:1–5
Parable of the barren fig tree	13:6–9
Woman healed on Sabbath	13:10–17
Man with dropsy healed	14:1–6
Lesson to guests and host	14:7–14
Count the cost	14:28–33
Parable of the lost coin	15:8–10
Parable of the lost son	15:11–32
Parable of the dishonest steward	16:1–13
Rich man and Lazarus	16:19–31
Unworthy servants	17:7–10
Ten lepers cleansed	17:11–19
Parable of the widow and the judge	18:1–8
Parable of the Pharisee and tax collector	18:9–14
Zacchaeus	19:1–10
The two swords	22:35–38
Jesus before Herod	23:6–12
Emmaus Road	24:13–35
Jesus' last words (according to Luke)	24:44–49
Ascension (Mark 16:19–20?)	24:50–53

Much of the above is assigned to the hypothetical source L.

*Some MSS read "seventy."

Synoptic Parallels

	Matthew	Mark	Luke	John
Preaching of John the Baptist	3:1–2	1:1–8	3:1–20	1:19–28
Baptism of Jesus	3:13–17	1:9–11	3:21–22	
Temptation	4:1–11	1:12–13	4:1–13	
Beginning of Galilee ministry	4:12–17	1:14–15	4:14–15	
Rejection at Nazareth	13:53–58	6:1–6	4:16–30	
Healing of Peter's mother-in-law and others	8:14–17	1:29–34	4:38–41	
Cleansing of a leper	8:1–4	1:40–45	5:12–16	
Healing of the paralytic	9:1–8	2:1–12	5:17–26	
Calling of Levi	9:9–13	2:13–17	5:27–32	
Fasting	9:14–17	2:18–22	5:33–39	
Grain plucking on the Sabbath	12:1–8	2:23–28	6:1–5	
Healing of withered hand	12:9–14	3:1–6	6:6–11	
Choosing of the Twelve	10:1–4	3:13–19	6:12–16	
Parable of the sower	13:1–23	4:1–20	8:4–15	
Jesus' true family	12:46–50	3:31–35	8:19–21	
Calming of a storm	8:23–27	4:35–41	8:22–25	
Healing of demon-possessed man	8:28–34	5:1–20	8:26–39	
Jairus's daughter and woman with hemorrhage	9:18–26	5:21–43	8:40–56	
The Twelve sent out	10:5–15	6:7–13	9:1–6	
John the Baptist beheaded	14:1–12	6:14–29	9:7–9	
Five thousand fed	14:13–21	6:30–44	9:10–17	6:1–14
Peter's confession	16:13–19	8:27–29	9:18–20	
Jesus' foretelling of death and resurrection	16:20–28	8:30–9:1	9:21–27	
Transfiguration	17:1–8	9:2–8	9:28–36	
Casting out of unclean spirits	17:14–18	9:14–27	9:37–43	
Second Prediction of death and resurrection	17:22–23	9:30–32	9:43–45	
"Who is greatest?"	18:1–5	9:33–37	9:46–48	
Jesus and Beelzebub	12:22–30	3:20–27	11:14–23	
Demand for a sign	12:38–42	8:11–12	11:29–32	
Parable of the mustard seed	13:31–32	4:30–32	13:18–19	
Blessing of little children	19:13–15	10:13–16	18:15–17	
Rich young ruler	19:16–30	10:17–31	18:18–30	
Third Prediction of death and resurrection	20:17–19	10:32–34	18:31–34	
Healing of blind Bartimaeus (and another)	20:29–34	10:46–52	18:35–42	
The Final Week				
Triumphal entry into Jerusalem	21:1–11	11:1–11	19:28–40	12:12–19
"By what authority …?"	21:23–27	11:27–33	20:1–8	
Vineyard and tenants	21:33–46	12:1–12	20:9–19	
"Render to Caesar"	22:15–22	12:13–17	20:20–26	
The resurrection	22:23–33	12:18–27	20:27–40	
David's son	22:41–46	12:35–37	20:41–44	
Sermon on the last days	24:1–36	13:1–32	21:5–33	
Passover plot	26:1–5, 14–16	14:1–2, 10–11	22:1–6	
Preparing of Passover	26:17–20	14:12–17	22:7–14	
Foretelling of betrayal	26:21–25	14:18–21	22:21–23	13:21–30
The Lord's Supper	26:26–30	14:22–26	22:14–20	
Prediction of Peter's denial	26:31–35	14:27–31	22:31–34	13:36–38
Gethsemane	26:36–46	14:32–42	22:39–46	
Arrest of Jesus	26:47–56	14:43–50	22:47–53	18:3–12
Sanhedrin (Peter's denial)	26:57–75	14:53–72	22:54–71	18:13–27
Jesus before Pilate	27:1–2, 11–14	15:1–5	23:1–5	18:28–38
Sentencing of Jesus	27:15–26	15:6–15	23:17–25	18:39–19:16
Crucifixion, Death, Burial	27:32–61	15:21–47	23:26–56	19:27–42
Resurrection	28:1–8	16:1–8	24:1–12	20:1–10

Matthew-Mark Parallels[1]

	Matthew	Mark
Call of the first disciples	4:18–22	1:16–20
Healing of possessed men	8:28–35	5:1–20
Death of John the Baptist	14:5–12	6:19–29
Crossing of the sea	14:22–23	6:45–52
Healing of sick in Gennesaret	14:34–36	6:53–56
Traditions and commandments	15:1–13	7:1–16
Explanation of defilement parable	15:15–20	7:17–23
Faith of Canaanite woman	15:21–28	7:24–30
Healings around Sea of Galilee	15:29–31	7:31–37
Jesus feeds four thousand	15:32–39	8:1–10
Religious leaders asking for a sign	16:1	8:11–12a
The sign of Jonah	16:4	8:12b–13
Identification of the new Elijah	17:9–13	9:9–13
Teaching about divorce	19:1–12	10:1–12
Laying on of hands	19:15	10:16
Cursing of the fig tree	21:18–19	11:12–14
Explanation of fig tree	21:20–22	11:20–26
Warning about false christs	24:23–25	13:21–23
Warning about vigilance	24:42	13:33–37
Anointing of Jesus at Bethany	26:6–13	14:3–9
Mocking of Jesus	27:27–31	15:16–20

[1] These parallels are those identified by A. M. Honoré, "A Statistical Study of the Synoptic Problem," in *The Synoptic Problem and Q: Selected Studies from Novum Testamentum*, ed. David E. Orton (Boston: Brill, 1999), 112-13.

Luke-Mark Parallels[1]

	Luke	Mark
Jesus preaching in synagogues	4:42–43	1:35–38
A lamp under a jar	8:16–18a	4:21–24
Instructions to the twelve	9:2–6	6:8–13
Anyone not against us is for us	9:49–50	9:38–41
Condemnation of scribes	20:47	12:40
Widow's offering	21:1–4	12:41–44

[1] These parallels are those identified by A. M. Honoré, "A Statistical Study of the Synoptic Problem," in *The Synoptic Problem and Q: Selected Studies from Novum Testamentum*, ed. David E. Orton (Boston: Brill, 1999), 114.

A Comparative Chart of the Four Gospels

The Gospels	Matthew	Mark	Luke	John
Probable date of writing	40–60	late 50s or early 60s	60–62	late 80s or early 90s
Probable place of writing	Antioch of Syria	Rome	Rome	Ephesus
Probable addressees	Jews in Syria	Christian Romans	Roman officials interested in Christianity, other cultured gentile Christians	Christians and/or non-Christians in the region around Ephesus
Presentation of Jesus Christ	Messiah-King, Son of David	Servant of Yahweh; the Redeemer	Fully human; compassionate, ideal man	Son of God; the Christ

Contrasts between the Synoptics and John

The Synoptics	The Gospel of John
Chiefly concerned with Jesus' ministry in the north, around Galilee	Gives more coverage to Jesus' ministry in the south, around Judea
Much emphasis on the kingdom	More emphasis on the person of Jesus
Jesus as Son of David, Son of Man	Jesus especially as Son of God and God Himself
Anticipation of the church and references to the infant church	Gospel of the maturing church
The earthly story	The heavenly meaning
Jesus' sayings generally short (e.g., parables)	More of the long discourses of Jesus
Comparatively little commentary by the gospel writers	Much commentary by John
Only one mention of a Passover	Mention of three, possibly four, Passovers

Adapted from Irving Jensen, *John* (Chicago: Moody, 1970), by permission.

The Five Gospels of the Jesus Seminar

The Jesus Seminar is a group of religious and biblical scholars founded in 1985 by Robert Funk and John Dominic Crossan under the auspices of the Westar Institute. Using the historical-critical method to focus on the quest for the historical Jesus, the seminar conducts workshops and has produced new translations of the New Testament and various apocryphal books.

Voting Procedure

Fellows of the Jesus Seminar were permitted to vote on the authenticity of the sayings of Jesus according to either of the following two options:[1]

Option 1		Option 2	
Red	I would include this item unequivocally in the database for determining who Jesus was.	Red	Jesus undoubtedly said this or something very much like it.
Pink	I would include this item with reservations (or modifications) in the database.	Pink	Jesus probably said something like this.
Gray	I would not include this item in the database, but I might make use of some of the content in determining who Jesus was.	Gray	Jesus did not say this, but the ideas contained in it are close to his own.
Black	I would not include this item in the primary database.	Black	Jesus did not say this; it represents the perspective or content of a later or different tradition.

Overall Results

Red and Pink sayings	Approximately 18% of the sayings of Jesus in Matthew, Mark, Luke, John, and Thomas received a red or pink rating.
Gray or Black sayings	The remaining 82% of Jesus' sayings recording in Matthew, Mark, Luke, John, and Thomas received a gray or black rating.

Results by Gospel

Matthew	17% of the sayings in Matthew were voted red or pink.
Mark	11% of the sayings in Mark were voted red or pink.
Luke	20% of the sayings in Luke were voted red or pink.
John	<1% of the sayings in John were voted red or pink.
Thomas	18% of the sayings in Thomas were voted red or pink.

Criteria of Authenticity[2]

Dissimilarity	If a saying is unlike Judaism or the practice of the early church, that saying may go back to Jesus.
Multiple Attestation	If a saying appears in Matthew or Luke and also appears in Q, Thomas, or Mark, that saying likely goes back to Jesus.
Coherence	If a saying coheres with the body of sayings that pass the tests of dissimilarity and multiple attestation, that saying may go back to Jesus.

[1] Robert W. Funk, Roy W. Hoover, and the Jesus Seminar, *The Five Gospels: The Search for the Authentic Words of Jesus* (New York: Polebridge Press, 1993), 36.

[2] Darrell L. Bock, "The Words of Jesus in the Gospels: Live, Jive, or Memorex?" in *Jesus Under Fire*, eds. Michael J. Wilkins and J. P. Moreland (Grand Rapids: Zondervan, 1995), 90–93.

The Genealogy of Jesus Christ

Genesis 5 and 11	1 Chronicles 1–3	Luke 3:23–38 (physical ancestry of Mary attributed to Joseph, by which Christ was of the seed of David)	Matthew 1 (legal ancestry of Joseph through which Christ was heir to David's throne)
Adam	Adam	Adam	
Seth	Seth	Seth	
Enosh	Enosh	Enos	
Kenan	Kenan	Cainan	
Mahalalel	Mahalalel	Mahalaleel	
Jared	Jared	Jared	
Enoch	Enoch	Enoch	
Methuselah	Methuselah	Methuselah	
Lamech	Lamech	Lamech	
Noah	Noah	Noah	
Shem	Shem	Shem	
Arphaxad	Arphaxad	Arphaxad	
		Cainan	
Shelah	Shelah	Shelah	
Eber	Eber	Eber	
Peleg	Peleg	Peleg	
Reu	Reu	Reu	
Serug	Serug	Serug	
Nahor	Nahor	Nahor	
Terah	Terah	Terah	
Abram	Abram	Abraham	Abraham
	Isaac	Isaac	Isaac
	Israel	Jacob	Jacob
	Judah	Judah	Judah
	Perez	Perez	Perez
	Hezron	Hezron	Hezron
	Ram	Ram	Ram
	Amminadab	Amminadab	Amminadab
	Nahshon	Nahshon	Nahshon
	Salmon	Salmon	Salmon
	Boaz	Boaz	Boaz
	Obed	Obed	Obed
	Jesse	Jesse	Jesse
	David	David	David
	Solomon	Nathan	Solomon
	Rehoboam	Mattatha	Rehoboam
	Abijah	Menna	Abijah

Genesis 5 and 11	1 Chronicles 1–3	Luke 3:23–38 (physical ancestry of Mary attributed to Joseph, by which Christ was of the seed of David)	Matthew 1 (legal ancestry of Joseph through which Christ was heir to David's throne)
	Asa	Melea	Asa
	Jehoshaphat	Eliakim	Jehoshaphat
	Jehoram	Jonam	Joram
	Ahaziah	Joseph	Uzziah
	Joash	Judah	
	Amaziah	Simeon	
	Azariah	Levi	
	Jotham	Matthat	Jotham
	Ahaz	Jorim	Ahaz
	Hezekiah	Eliezer	Hezekiah
	Manasseh	Joshua	Manasseh
	Amon	Er	Amon
	Josiah	Elmadam	Josiah
	Jehoiakim	Cosam	
	Jehoiachin	Addi	Jeconiah
	(Jeconiah is a	Melki	
	variant spelling)	Neri	
	Shealtiel	Shealtiel	Shealtiel
	Pedaiah		
	Zerubbabel	Zerubbabel	Zerubbabel
		Rhesa	Abiud
		Joanan	Eliakim
		Joda	Azor
		Josech	Zadok
		Semein	Akim
		Mattathias	Eliud
		Maath	Eleazar
		Naggai	Matthan
		Esli	Jacob
		Nahum	
		Amos	
		Mattathias	
		Joseph	
		Jannai	
		Melki	
		Levi	
		Matthat	
		Heli	
		(Joseph) Mary	Joseph (Mary)
		Jesus	Jesus

Old Testament Prophecies concerning Christ and Christianity

OT Reference	NT Citation	Subject Matter of Fulfilled Prophecy
Ps. 2:7	Acts 13:33; Heb. 1:5; 5:5	The divine sonship of Christ
Ps. 40:6–8	Heb. 10:5–9	The incarnation
1. Ps. 110:1 2. 2 Sam. 7:12 (Ps. 89:3–4)[1]; Mic. 5:2	1. *Matt. 22:43–44; Mark 12:36; Luke 20:42–43*[2] 2. John 7:42	The Davidic descent of Christ
Isa. 7:14 (8:8, 10—LXX)	Matt. 1:21–23	The virgin conception of Christ
Mic. 5:2 (2 Sam. 5:2; 1 Chron. 11:2)	Matt. 2:6; John 7:42	The birth of Christ in Bethlehem
Hos. 11:1	Matt. 2:15	The flight to Egypt
Jer. 31:15	Matt. 2:16–18	The killing of the innocent children by Herod
unknown	Matt. 2:23	The return to Nazareth
Isa. 40:3–5	Matt. 3:3; Mark 1:3; Luke 3:4–6; John 1:23	The ministry of John the Baptist in the wilderness
Mal. 3:1; Isa. 40:3	Mark 1:22; Luke 7:27	John the Baptist as the forerunner of Yahweh
Mal. 4:5–6	*Matt. 11:14; 17:12; Mark 9:12–13*; Luke 1:17	John the Baptist as the prophesied Elijah
Ps. 69:9	John 2:17	The cleansing of the temple
Isa. 9:1–2	Matt. 4:14–16	The ministry of Christ in Capernaum
Deut. 18:15–16, 1a	Acts 3:22–23; 7:37	The prophetic ministry of Christ
1. Isa. 61:1–2 2. Isa. 42:1–4	1. *Luke 4:18–21* 2. Matt. 12:17–21	Christ's ministry of compassion
Isa. 53:4	Matt. 8:17	Christ's ministry of healing
Ps. 110:4	Heb. 5:6; 7:17, 21	The eternal priesthood of Christ

[1] Verses in parentheses are not directly related to the topic.

[2] References that are italicized are statements by Christ.

OT Reference	NT Citation	Subject Matter of Fulfilled Prophecy
Ps. 78:2	Matt. 13:35	Christ's use of parables
1. Isa. 6:9–10 2. Isa. 53:1; 6:9–10	1. *Matt. 13:14–15;* *Mark 4:12; Luke 8:10* 2. John 12:37–41	The hardening of many who heard Christ
(Isa. 62:11) Zech. 9:9	Matt. 21:5; John 12:14–15	The triumphal entry of Christ on a young donkey
1. Ps. 118:22–23 2. Ps. 118:22 3. Ps. 118:22; Isa. 8:14	1. *Matt. 21:42;* *Mark 12:10–11;* *Luke 20:17* 2. Acts 4:11 3. 1 Peter 2:7–8	The rejection of Christ by the Jews
Ps. 35:19; 69:4	*John 15:25*	The hatred of the Jews (?)
Ps. 22:1–18; Isa. 53:3ff.	*Mark 9:12;* *Luke 18:32; 24:25, 46a*	The suffering of Christ
Zech. 13:7	*Matt. 26:31; Mark 14:27*	The cowardice of the disciples
Ps. 41:9 (109:4–5, 7–8?)	*John 13:18; 17:12*	The betrayal by Judas
Zech. 11:12–13	Matt. 27:9–10	The end of Judas
Zech. 13:7	*Matt. 26:54–56; Mark 14:48–49*	The arrest of Christ
Isa. 53:12	*Luke 22:37*	Christ accounted as a transgressor
unknown	*Luke 18:32*	The sufferings of Christ at the hands of the Gentiles
Ps. 2:1–2	Acts 4:25–27	The conspiracy against Christ
Ps. 22:18	John 19:24	The casting of lots over the clothes of Jesus
Ps. 22:15	John 19:28	Christ's thirst on the cross
Ps. 34:20 (Exod. 12:46; Num. 9:12)	John 19:36	Christ's bones not being broken
Zech. 12:10	John 19:37	Christ's pierced side

OT Reference	NT Citation	Subject Matter of Fulfilled Prophecy
1. Isa. 53:7–8 (LXX); 53:8–9 2. Deut. 21:23	1. Luke 18:32; Acts 8:32–35; 1 Cor. 15:3 2. Gal. 3:13	The death of Christ
1. Ps. 16:8–11; 2 Sam. 22:6–7; Ps. 18:4–6; 116:3 (last three identical) 2. 2 Sam. 7:12–13; Ps. 132:11 3. Hos. 6:2(?)	1. Acts 2:25–28 2. Acts 2:30–31 3. *Luke 18:33; 24:46;* John 2:19–22; 1 Cor. 15:4	The resurrection of Christ
Ps. 110:1; 2:7; 68:18	Acts 2:34–35; 13:33–35; Eph. 4:8	The ascension of Christ
1. Ps. 110:1 2. Ps. 2:8–9	1. *Matt. 22:43–44; Mark 12:36;* *Luke 20:42–43;* Acts 2:34–35; Heb. 1:13 2. Rev. 2:27	The exaltation of Christ
Ps. 109:8; 69:25	Acts 1:20	The replacement of Judas
Joel 2:28–32 (3:1–5—LXX)	Acts 2:17–21	The outpouring of the Holy Spirit at Pentecost
1. Isa. 49:6 2. Amos 9:11–12 3. Hos. 2:23; 1:10 4. Deut. 32:43; 2 Sam 22:50; Ps. 18:49; 117:1; Isa. 11:10 5. Gen. 12:3; 18:18; 22:18 6. Isa. 54:1	1. *Luke 24:47;* Acts 13:47 2. Acts 15:14–18 3. Rom. 9:25–26 4. Rom. 15:9–12 5. Gal. 3:8 6. Gal. 4:27	The universal expansion of the gospel
1. Isa. 6:9–10 2. Deut. 29:4; Ps. 35:8; 69:22–23 (Isa. 29:10); Isa. 10:22–23 (Hos. 1:10)	1. Acts 28:26–27 2. Rom. 9:27, 33; 11:8–10	The hardening of the Jews against the gospel
Ps. 44:22	Rom. 8:36	The persecution of Christians
1. Exod. 29:45; Lev. 26:12; Ezek. 37:27 (Isa. 52:11; Jer. 32:38; Ezek. 20:34) 2. Jer. 31:33–34 3. Jer. 31:33–34	1. 2 Cor. 6:16–18 2. Heb. 8:8–12 3. Heb. 10:16–17	The blessings of the new covenant
Ps. 22:22; Isa. 8:17—LXX; 8:18	Heb. 2:12–13	Christ's viewing of believers as His brothers

The Jewish Enthronement Motif and Jesus the Messiah

OT Event	Parallel with Jesus the Messiah	Scripture
Choice of messiah 1 Sam. 9:16; 16:1; Ps. 89:20a	Prophecy in the Old Testament	Isa. 7:14; 9:6–7
Anointing of Messiah 1 Sam. 10:1; 16:1, 13; 2 Sam. 5:3; 1 Kings 1:34, 38–39; 2 Kings 9:1–3	Baptism by John	Matt. 3:13–17; Acts 2:36 (Christos, the anointed one); Heb. 1:9
Declaration of sonship 2 Sam. 7:14; 1 Chron. 22:10; 28:6; Ps. 2:7; 89:26–29	Baptism; Resurrection	Matt. 3:17; Rom. 1:4; Heb. 1:5; 5:5
Ascension to the throne Ps. 110:1a	Ascensions to the heavenly throne	Acts 2:30ff; Eph. 1:20; Heb. 1:3, 13
Reign with Yahweh Ps. 2:6; 45:6; 89:3–4	Present reign with the Father	Acts 2:36; Heb. 1:13; 1 Peter 3:22
Conquering of enemies Ps. 2:8ff.; 89:21ff.; 110:1b–3, 5–7	Second Coming	Acts 2:34–35

A Chronology of the Ministry of Jesus

Event	Time	Place	Matthew	Mark	Luke	John
From Beginning to Final Week:						
Jesus is baptized	c. A.D. 26	Jordan River	3:13–17	1:9–11	3:21–23	1:29–39
Jesus is tempted by Satan		Wilderness	4:1–11	1:12–13	4:1–13	
Jesus performs His first miracle	27	Cana				2:1–11
Jesus and Nicodemus converse		Judea				3:1–21
Jesus talks to the Samaritan woman		Samaria				4:5–42
Jesus heals a nobleman's son		Cana				4:46–54
Jesus attends an unknown feast and disputes with the Jewish leadership	?	Jerusalem			4:16–31	5:1–47
The people of Jesus' hometown try to kill Him		Nazareth				
Four fishermen become Jesus' followers		Sea of Galilee	4:18–22	1:16–20	5:1–11	
Jesus heals Peter's mother-in-law		Capernaum	8:14–17	1:29–34	4:38–41	
Jesus begins His first preaching trip through Galilee		Galilee	4:23–25	1:35–39	4:42–44	
Matthew decides to follow Jesus		Capernaum	9:9–13	2:13–17	5:27–32	
Jesus chooses the Twelve	28			3:13–19	6:12–15	
Jesus preaches the "Sermon on the Mount"			5:1–7:29		6:20–49	
A sinful woman anoints Jesus		Capernaum			7:36–50	
Jesus travels again through Galilee					8:1–3	
Jesus tells parables about the kingdom			13:1–52	4:1–34	8:4–18	
Jesus quiets the storm		Sea of Galilee	8:23–27	4:35–41	8:22–25	
Jairus's daughter is brought back to life by Jesus		Capernaum	9:18–26	5:21–43	8:40–56	
Jesus sends the Twelve out to preach and heal			9:35–11:1	6:6–13	9:1–6	
John the Baptist is killed by Herod		Machaerus	14:1–12	6:14–29	9:7–9	
Jesus feeds 5,000 people	Spring 29	Near Bethsaida	14:13–21	6:30–44	9:10–17	6:1–14
Jesus walks on water			14:22–23	6:45–52		6:16–21
Jesus feeds 4,000 people	Later in the year		15:32–39	8:1–9		
Peter says that Jesus is the Son of God		Caesarea Philippi	16:13–20	8:27–30	9:18–21	
Jesus tells His disciples He is going to die soon			16:21–26	8:31–37	9:22–25	
Jesus is transfigured			17:1–13	9:2–13	9:28–36	
Jesus pays His temple taxes		Capernaum	17:24–27			
Jesus attends the Feast of Tabernacles	October 29	Jerusalem				7:11–52
Jesus heals a man who was born blind	Later in the year	Jerusalem				9:1–41

Event	Place	Time	Matthew	Mark	Luke	John
Jesus visits Mary and Martha	Bethany	Winter 29			10:38–42	11:1–44
Jesus raises Lazarus from the dead	Bethany	30				
Jesus begins His last trip to Jerusalem	Across the Jordan				9:51	
Jesus blesses the little children	Across the Jordan		19:13–16	10:13–16	18:15–17	
Jesus talks to the rich young man	Near the Jordan		19:16–30	10:17–31	18:18–30	
Jesus again tells about His death and resurrection	Jericho		20:17–19	10:32–34	18:31–34	
Jesus heals blind Bartimaeus	Jericho		20:29–34	10:46–52	18:35–43	
Jesus talks to Zacchaeus					19:1–10	
Jesus returns to Bethany to visit Mary and Martha	Bethany	Friday				11:55–12:1
The Final Week:						
Mary anoints Jesus	Jerusalem	Saturday	26:6–13	14:3–9		12:2–8
Jesus enters Jerusalem on a donkey	Jerusalem	Sunday	21:1–17	11:1–11	19:29–44	
Jesus curses the fig tree	Jerusalem	Monday	21:18–19	11:12–14		
Jesus cleanses the temple	Jerusalem	Monday	21:12–13	11:15–18	19:45–46	
Jesus' authority is questioned	Jerusalem	Tuesday	21:23–22:14	11:27–12:12	20:1–19	
Jesus teaches in the temple	Jerusalem	Tuesday	22:41–46	12:35–37	20:41–44	
There is a plot to betray Jesus	Jerusalem	Wednesday (?)	26:14–16	14:10–11	22:3–6	
Jesus and His disciples eat Last Supper	Jerusalem	Thursday	26:17–25	14:12–21	22:7–30	13:1–30
Jesus gives His farewell discourse	Jerusalem	Thursday				14–16
Jesus prays in Gethsemane	Jerusalem	Thursday	26:30–46	14:26–42	22:39–46	18:1
Jesus is arrested and is tried by the Sanhedrin	Jerusalem	Friday	26:47–27:1	14:43–15:1	22:47–71	18:2–27
Jesus is tried by Pilate	Jerusalem	Friday	27:2–26	15:1–15	23:1–25	18:28–19:16
Jesus is crucified	Jerusalem	Friday	27:31–56	15:20–46	23:26–49	19:16–30
Jesus is buried	Jerusalem	Friday–Sunday	27:57–66	15:42–47	23:50–56	19:31–42
After the Resurrection:						
The tomb is seen to be empty	Jerusalem	Sunday	28:1–10	16:1–8[1]	24:1–12	20:1–10
Mary Magdalene sees Jesus in the garden	Jerusalem	Sunday		16:9–11		20:11–18
Jesus appears to the two going to Emmaus		Sunday		16:12–13	24:13–35	
Jesus appears to ten disciples	Jerusalem	Sunday			24:36–43	20:19–25
Jesus appears to the Eleven	Jerusalem	One week later		16:14		20:26–31
Jesus talks with some of His disciples	Sea of Galilee					21:1–25
Jesus returns to His Father in heaven	Mt. of Olives	Forty days later	28:16–20	16:19–20	24:44–53	

Adapted from the *New International Version of the Holy Bible, Illustrated Children's Edition* (Grand Rapids: Zondervan, 1975), by permission.

[1] There is a question of authenticity regarding these references in Mark 16.

An Alternate Chronological Table of Christ's Life

Christ's birth	winter 5/4 B.C.
Herod the Great's death	March/April 4 B.C.
Prefects began to rule over Judea and Samaria	A.D. 6
Christ at the temple when twelve	Passover, April 29, 9
Caiaphas became high priest	A.D. 18
Pilate arrived in Judea	A.D. 26
Commencement of John the Baptist's ministry	A.D. 29
Commencement of Christ's ministry	summer/autumn A.D. 29
Christ's first Passover (John 2:13)	April 7, 30
John the Baptist imprisoned	A.D. 30 or 31
Christ's second Passover	April 23, 31
John the Baptist's death	A.D. 31 or 32
Christ at the Feast of Tabernacles (John 5:1)	October 21–28, 31
Christ's third Passover (John 6:4)	April 13/14, 32
Christ at the Feast of Tabernacles (John 7:2, 10)	September 10–17, 32
Christ at the Feast of Dedication (John 10:22–39)	December 18, 32
Christ's final week	March 28–April 5, 33
Arrived at Bethany	Saturday, March 28
Crowds at Bethany	Sunday, March 29
Triumphal entry	Monday, March 30
Cursed fig tree and cleansed temple	Tuesday, March 31
Temple controversy and Olivet discourse	Wednesday, April 1
Christ ate Passover, was betrayed, arrested, and tried	Thursday, April 2
Christ tried and crucified	Friday, April 3
Christ laid in the tomb	Saturday, April 4
Christ resurrected	Sunday, April 5
Christ's ascension (Acts 1)	Thursday, May 14, 33
Day of Pentecost (Acts 2)	Sunday, May 24, 33

Adapted from Harold Hoehner, *Chronological Aspects of the Life of Christ* (Grand Rapids: Zondervan, 1977), by permission.

The Ministry of Christ

Hoehner Event	Hoehner Year	Stevens & Burton Event	Stevens & Burton Year	Cheney Event	Cheney Year	Stauffer Event	Stauffer Year
John the Baptist's ministry begins Jesus' ministry begins (summer/fall)	29	John the Baptist's ministry begins Jesus' ministry begins	26	John the Baptist's ministry begins	28	John the Baptist's ministry begins	28
First Passover (John 2:13) John the Baptist imprisoned	30	First Passover (John 2:13) John the Baptist imprisoned	27	First Passover (John 2:13) Jesus' ministry begins with the cleansing of the temple	29	First Passover (John 1:29, 41ff.) Jesus' ministry begins	29
Second Passover (not mentioned) Feast of Tabernacles (John 5:1) John the Baptist beheaded	31	Second Passover (not mentioned) Feast of Tabernacles John the Baptist beheaded	28	Second Passover Allusion in Luke 6:1 Feast of Tabernacles John the Baptist beheaded	30	Second Passover (John 2:13, 23) John the Baptist imprisoned	30
Third Passover (John 6:4) Feast of Tabernacles (John 7:2) Feast of Dedication (John 10:22)	32	Third Passover (John 6:4) Feast of Tabernacles Feast of Dedication	29	Third Passover (John 6:4) Feast of Tabernacles Feast of Dedication	31	Third Passover (not mentioned) Feast of Tabernacles John the Baptist beheaded	31
Fourth Passover (John 11:55) Christ crucified, Friday, April 3 Christ resurrected, Sunday, April 5	33	Fourth Passover (John 11:55) Christ crucified Christ resurrected	30	Fourth Passover Alluded to in story of temple tax of Matthew 17:24 and the massacre and sacrifices in Luke 13:1	32	Fourth Passover (John 6:4) Feast of Tabernacles Feast of Dedication	32
				Fifth Passover (John 11:55) Christ crucified Christ resurrected	33	Fifth Passover (John 11:55) Christ crucified Christ resurrected	33

Sources: Harold Hoehner, *Chronological Aspects of the Life of Christ* (Grand Rapids: Zondervan, 1977); W. M. Arnold Stevens and Ernest Dewitt Burton, *A Harmony of the Gospels: For Historical Study* (New York: Charles Scribner's Sons, 1905); Johnson M. Cheney, *The Life of Christ in Stereo* (Portland, OR: Western Baptist Seminary Press, 1969); Ethelbert Stauffer, trans. Dorothea M. Barton, *Jesus and His Story* (London: SCM Press, 1960).

The Duration of Christ's Ministry

One Year	
Evidence	**Reply**
1. Luke 4:19 speaks of the acceptable *year* of the Lord (Isa. 61:2).	1. Isa. 61:2 was quoted to announce the arrival of Messiah, not to give the duration of His ministry. Year is not to be taken as a reference to a solar year.
2. Christ's ministry fits in between the disciples' plucking grain (Mark 2:23) and the Passover mentioned in Mark 14:1.	2. This does not allow for the number of events that took place during Christ's life. The ministry of Jesus is too compressed by the one-year theory.
3. The Synoptics mention only one Passover, that of Passion week.	3. The gospel of John speaks of at least three (2:13; 6:4; 11:55).
4. John 6:4 is not the Passover (some MSS omit "the Passover") but instead possibly Tabernacles.	4. "The Passover" is the better textual reading. The feast would not be Tabernacles (autumn), since 6:10 mentions green grass (spring) and so most likely the Passover.
Advocates: Valentinus, Clement of Alexandria, Origen, Johannes Belser, Hermann von Soden, Joseph Klausner, Maurice Goguel, A. T. Olmstead, Hans Conzelmann (?).	

Two Years	
Evidence	**Reply**
1. The gospel of John specifically mentions three Passovers (2:13; 6:4; 11:55); so Jesus' ministry lasted at least two years.	1. More than two years may be understood with three Passovers if a year is understood between John 2:13 and 6:4. There also may be more than three Passovers.
2. John 5 and 6 should be transposed in order to make better geographical sense: At the end of John 4 Jesus is in Cana of Galilee. In chapter 6 He is by the Sea of Galilee. In chapter 5 He goes up to Jerusalem, and in chapter 7 Jesus can no longer travel in Judea; so He traveled to Galilee. The feast of John 5:1 is thought to be the Passover mentioned in John 6:4.	2. There is no textual support for the transposition. In fact John 5:19–47, in which Christ's divine sonship is established, furnishes a foundation for His claims in chapter 6. Moreover, John 7:3 seems to indicate that Jesus had not recently been in Jerusalem performing miracles, and this would be incongruous if chapter 7 came immediately after chapter 5.

Evidence	Reply
Chart of Transposition	
<table><tr><td>4 Cana of Galilee 5 Jerusalem (feast) 6 Sea of Galilee (approaching Passover) 7 Recently left Judea for Galilee</td><td>4 Cana of Galilee 6 Sea of Galilee (Passover approaching 6:4) 5 Jerusalem (feast of v. 1 is Passover) 7 Recently left Judea for Galilee</td></tr></table>	
Advocates: Apollinaris, Epiphanius, Edmund F. Sutcliffe, Josef Blinzler, George B. Caird, Eugen Ruckstuhl, Rudolf Schnackenburg, F. F. Bruce, George B. Duncan.	

Three Years

Evidence	Reply
1. In addition to the three Passovers explicitly mentioned in the gospel of John (2:13; 6:4; 11:55), an additional year should be understood between the Passovers mentioned in 2:13 and 6:4. Not all the feasts are mentioned in John (e.g., Feast of Pentecost). Also, the Synoptic accounts require another year between the Passovers of 2:13 and 6:4; e.g., Mark 6:39 indicates springtime but Mark 2:23 points to a harvest season a year earlier. John 2:13 was in Judea, but Mark 6:39 was in Galilee, too close to be the same Passover.	1. There is no mention of an additional Passover by John. Since John mentioned three Passovers, one would expect the mention of a fourth if one occurred.
2. John 4:35 says there are but four months to harvest. This should be taken as a seasonal indicator. This places Jesus in Samaria in January/February after the Passover of John 2:13, allowing for the Passover between John 2:13 and 6:4.	2. The saying is a proverb rather than a statement of fact. Too many events are compressed into the last six months of Jesus' ministry.
Advocates: Melito, Eusebius, George Ogg, A. T. Robertson, William Armstrong, William Hendriksen, Leslie W. P. Madison, Donald Guthrie, Harold Hoehner.	

Four Years	
Evidence	**Reply**
1. There are five Passovers in the ministry of Jesus.	1. Only three or four Passovers are indicated.
2. A four-year ministry allows for a more relaxed time in the last six months.	2. The ministry of Jesus in the last few months may have been rushed, but this is not unreasonable.
3. The departure of Jesus to Jerusalem in John 7 (a few days) is different from that in Luke 9:51 (several months).	3. The three journeys in John (7:2; 11:7, 17–18; 11:55) and Luke (9:51; 13:22; 17:11) probably correspond.
4. There is an extra Passover either before John 2:13 (and another between 2:13 and 6:4) or between 2:13 and 6:4 (and another between 6:4 and 11:55).	4. There is no indication that John 1:29ff. was in Passover season or that Jesus went to Jerusalem (cf. John 1:28–29 and 1:43; 2:1). A year between John 10 and 11 (argued by Cheney) has no internal evidence. Though tax collectors came the month before Passover, Matt. 17:24–27 seems to indicate they came late. Also, the massacre and sacrifices of Luke 13:1 could fit the Passover of John 6:4.
5. Parable of the barren fig tree (Luke 13:6–9) indicates four-year ministry.	5. Too much is read from the parable. It is not seeking to teach about the duration of Jesus' ministry.
6. Luke 6:1 is said to refer to "the second First Sabbath" in Western and Byzantine texts and is compared with Lev. 23:15–21.	6. The variant reading of Luke 6:1 is highly questionable textually, and even the meaning of the phrase is much debated.
7. John 2–6 has two years without mention of a Passover; so may John 6–12.	7. John 2–6 has strong internal support, whereas John 6–12 does not.
Advocates: Ethelbert Stauffer, Johnston M. Cheney, Stanley A. Ellisen.	

Chart of Alternate Four-Year Views

Stauffer[1]	**Cheney**[2]
1st P. John 1:29, 41ff.	John 2:13
2nd P. John 2:13, 23	Luke 6:1, allusion
3rd P. not mentioned;	John 6:4
cf. John 4:35 (winter); 5:1 (autumn)	
4th P. John 6:4; 7:2 (autumn);	alluded to in Matt. 17:24 and Luke 13:1
10:22 (winter)	
5th P. John 11:55	John 11:15

[1] Ethelbert Stauffer, trans. Dorothea M. Barton, *Jesus and His Story* (London: SCM Press, 1960).

[2] Johnson M. Cheney, *The Life of Christ in Stereo* (Portland, OR: Western Baptist Seminary Press, 1969).

Parables of Jesus

Parable	Reference(s)	Type	Topic	Lesson[1]
Sower and the seed	Matt. 13:1–8; Mark 4:3–8; Luke 8:5–8	Didactic	Kingdom	Productivity within the kingdom depends on the kind of response to the Word one makes.
Weeds	Matt. 13:24–30	Didactic	Kingdom	Until the kingdom dominates, it will coexist in the world with the kingdom of Satan.
Mustard seed	Matt. 13:31–32; Mark 4:30–32; Luke 13:18–19	Didactic	Kingdom	Though the kingdom begins small, it will be large at the end.
Yeast	Matt. 13:33; Luke 13:20–21	Didactic	Kingdom	Though beginning small, the kingdom will dominate the earth one day.
Hidden treasure	Matt. 13:44	Didactic	Kingdom	Total commitment to the kingdom should be given because of its infinite worth.
Pearl of great price	Matt. 13:45–46	Didactic	Kingdom	Total commitment to the kingdom should be given because of its infinite worth.
Dragnet	Matt. 13:47–50	Didactic	Kingdom	Until the kingdom dominates, it will coexist in the world with the kingdom of Satan.
Growing seed	Mark 4:26–29	Didactic	Kingdom	God will bring about His kingdom apart from human effort.
Workers in the vineyard	Matt. 20:1–16	Didactic	Service	God grants grace to the undeserving out of His generosity.
Talents	Matt. 25:14–30	Didactic	Service	One must be prepared for the coming of Christ by commitment to service.
Ten minas	Luke 19:11–27	Didactic	Service	Disciples of Jesus are to remain faithful until He returns.

[1] The lessons from the parables differ among interpreters, but most of those given here are fairly certain.

Parable	Reference(s)	Type	Topic	Lesson
Unworthy servants	Luke 17:7–10	Didactic	Service	Disciples are not to expect gratitude for everything they do; service must come from a sense of mission.
Friend at midnight	Luke 11:5–8	Didactic	Prayer	If a neighbor will certainly help in time of need rather than bring shame on himself, how much more will God meet the needs of those who ask.[2]
Persistent widow (unjust judge)	Luke 18:1–8	Didactic	Prayer	If an unjust judge will give justice because of persistence, how much more will the just and gracious God make things right at the coming of Christ.
Lowest seat at the feast	Luke 14:16	Didactic	Humility	Disciples are to be exalted by God, not by themselves.
Pharisee and the tax collector	Luke 18:9–14	Didactic	Humility	God's forgiveness comes to the repentant, not the self-righteous.
Good Samaritan	Luke 10:30–37	Didactic	Love for neighbor	To love and help anyone who is in need, especially one's enemy, is being a neighbor.
Lost sheep	Matt. 18:12–14; Luke 15:3–7	Evangelical	God's concern for the lost	There is a universal need to repent.
Lost coin	Luke 15:8–10	Evangelical	God's concern for the lost	God rejoices over the repentance of one sinner.
Lost son	Luke 15:11–32	Evangelical	God's concern for the lost	All who repent are heirs of God's forgiving grace without distinction.
Two debtors	Luke 7:41–43	Evangelical	Gratitude of the redeemed	Gratitude over forgiveness is proportionate to the recognition of one's sinfulness.

[2] Cf. Alan F. Johnson, "Assurance for Man: The Fallacy of Translating *Anaidea* by 'Persistence' in Luke 11:5–8" in *Journal of the Evangelical Theological Society*, vol. 22, no. 2 (June 1979), 123–31, for this interpretation, which I believe is preferable to the usual interpretation that persistence brings results.

Parable	Reference(s)	Type	Topic	Lesson
Ten virgins	Matt. 25:1–13	Prophetic and judicial	Preparedness for Christ's return	Those who intend to meet Christ at His return must be prepared in view of the imminence of His coming.
Wise and wicked servants	Matt. 24:45–51; Luke 12:42–48	Prophetic and judicial	Preparedness for Christ's return	All true followers of Jesus will watch and be ready for His return.
Watchful porter	Mark 13:34–37	Prophetic and judicial	Preparedness for Christ's return	True followers of Jesus will watch and be ready for His return.
Two sons	Matt. 21:28–32	Prophetic and judicial	Judgment on Israel	The "irreligious" Jew who repents will enter the kingdom rather than the unfaithful Jewish leaders.
Tenants	Matt. 21:33–46; Mark 12:1–12; Luke 20:9–18	Prophetic and judicial	Judgment on Israel	In the present age God has transferred stewardship of His kingdom from unbelieving Israel to other stewards.
Barren fig tree	Luke 13:6–9	Prophetic and judicial	Judgment on Israel	Israel was receiving from God a last chance to repent, after which God would reject it.
Wedding banquet	Matt. 22:1–14	Prophetic and judicial	Judgment	All are invited into God's kingdom, but only the repentant will enjoy His blessings.
Unmerciful servant	Matt. 18:23–35	Prophetic and judicial	Judgment within the kingdom	Humans need to imitate the forgiveness of God.
Householder	Matt. 13:52			Disciples should be able to draw spiritual truths from the parables.
Shrewd manager	Luke 16:1–10			Disciples of Jesus must use money in acts of kindness, for such action will be beneficial in the future.
Rich man and Lazarus	Luke 16:19–31			One must establish proper priorities in this life in reference to God and money.

These are the major parables in the Gospels. Some would add others such as the patch and wineskins found in Matthew 9 and parallels. In addition, there are several passages, identified by the word *like*, that are possibly parables.

Nature Miracles

Miracle	Scripture	Where	To or for Whom	Why	Results
Turning water into wine	John 2:1–11	Cana	People of the wedding feast	To prove that He is the Son of God	This marked the beginning of Christ's miracles and the moment when the disciples began to believe in Him.
Feeding of five thousand	Matt. 14:15–21 Mark 6:35–44 Luke 9:12–17 John 6:5–15	Sea of Galilee (near Bethsaida)	Jews	To show compassion and the power of God	The people tried to make Him king to fulfill their physical needs. (John's gospel only).
Stilling the storm	Matt. 8:23–27 Mark 4:35–41 Luke 8:22–25	Sea of Galilee (between Capernaum and Gadara)	Disciples	To show that Jesus possessed the power of God and could deliver them from all danger. Also to challenge the disciples' faith.	Jesus was shown to have power over nature, and the disciples' faith was strengthened.
Walking on the sea	Matt. 14:22–33 Mark 6:45–52 John 6:16–21	Sea of Galilee (between Bethsaida and Capernaum)	Disciples	To show Jesus' divinity	Jesus' divinity was shown alongside Peter's lack of faith.
Providing tax money in fish's mouth	Matt. 17:24–27	Capernaum	Tax collectors	To avoid offending the tax collectors	The tax was paid.
Feeding of four thousand	Matt. 15:32–39 Mark 8:1–9	Near Bethsaida	Those who had been following Jesus into the wilderness	To feed those who had been following Him for three days	All ate, and seven baskets were filled with leftovers.
Withering of fig tree	Matt. 21:17–22 Mark 11:12–14, 20–25	On the journey from Bethany to Jerusalem	Disciples	To teach a lesson on faith and coming of destruction of Jerusalem	The tree withered, and Jesus taught the greatness of faith and the coming destruction of Jerusalem.
First catch of fish	Luke 5:1–11	Sea of Galilee	Especially Peter but also James and John	To explain to Peter that he should "catch men" from that time on	James, John, and Simon (Peter) followed Christ.
Second catch of fish	John 21:1–14	Sea of Tiberias	Seven disciples	Third appearance to the disciples to reconfirm His resurrection	They all recognized Him when they came ashore.

Healing Miracles

Miracle	Scripture	Where	To or for Whom	Why	Results
Healing of nobleman's son at Cana	John 4:46–54	Cana	Official of Capernaum	The official's request and faith in the Lord	The man and his whole household believed.
Restoring sight of blind man at Bethsaida	Mark 8:22–26	Bethsaida	Blind man	The desire of the people who brought him	Jesus healed him and told him to go home.
Restoring sight of man born blind	John 9:1–41	Jerusalem	Blind man in Jerusalem	"So that the work of God might be displayed in his life"	The man became a believer, and the Pharisees' guilt was revealed.
Raising of Lazarus	John 11:1–45	Bethany	Lazarus, Mary, and Martha	To show the work of God; so the people would believe that Jesus was sent by God; "I am Resurrection and life."	The Pharisees were afraid that many would believe in Christ and the Romans would take over their nation.
Curing of demon-possessed man (men)	Matt. 8:28–34 Mark 5:1–20 Luke 8:26–39	Gadara (east shore of Sea of Galilee)	Gadarenes	To send the demons out and to show that Jesus regularly overcame Satan's power	Because they were frightened, the people asked Him to leave. Also, the man was sent to tell what God had done for him.
Raising of Jairus's daughter	Matt. 9:18–26 Mark 5:22–24, 35–43 Luke 8:41–42, 49–56	Capernaum	Jairus—a synagogue ruler	Jairus's request and his great faith in the Lord	Jesus said to tell no one, but many were told.
Healing of invalid at Bethesda	John 5:1–18	Bethesda	Jewish man	The man's faith in the Lord	The man was made well and the Jews made a greater attempt to kill Jesus.

Miracle	Scripture	Where	To or for Whom	Why	Results
Curing of woman with twelve-year bleeding	Matt. 9:20–22 Mark 5:25–34 Luke 8:43–48	Capernaum	Woman with blood disease	The woman's great faith	She was made well. Many witnessed the event.
Restoring of paralytic at Capernaum	Matt. 9:1–8 Mark 2:1–12 Luke 5:17–26	Capernaum	Paralytic man	To show that He has power to perform miracles and forgive sins	The man praised God. Many around were more receptive and believing.
Curing of leper near Gennesaret	Matt. 8:1–4 Mark 1:40–45 Luke 5:12–15	Galilean city	Man with leprosy	His faith in Christ	Jesus told the man to tell only the priest and give an offering. The man told many, who then came to Jesus for physical needs.
Healing of Peter's mother-in-law	Matt. 8:14–17 Mark 1:29–31 Luke 4:38–39	Capernaum	Peter, Peter's mother-in-law	Compassion; friendship to Peter	Jesus healed her, and she rose and waited on Him.
Restoring of withered hand	Matt. 12:9–14 Mark 3:1–6 Luke 6:6–11	Synagogue in Galilee	Pharisees	To rebuke the scribes for trying to convict Him for healing on the Sabbath	The scribes planned to destroy Jesus.
Healing of child with demon	Matt. 17:14–20 Mark 9:14–29 Luke 9:37–43	Area of Mt. Tabor	Boy with a demon	To show the lack of faith in the people and the disciples	The disciples were shown how small their faith was and Jesus told them of the necessity of prayer.
Restoring blind and dumb demoniac	Matt. 12:22 Luke 11:14	Galilee	Pharisees	To prove to the Pharisees that Jesus was not working under the power of Beelzebub	Christ demonstrated that He did the works of God; the Pharisees hardened their hearts.
Giving sight to two blind men	Matt. 9:27–31	Capernaum	Two blind men	Their faith	The men spread the news of Christ's work for them.
Healing of dumb demoniac	Matt. 9:32–34	Capernaum	Dumb man possessed by a demon	To show that Jesus regularly overcame Satan's power	The Pharisees said He was working through demonic powers.
Healing of deaf-mute	Mark 7:31–37	Region of Decapolis	Deaf-mute	The desire of the people who brought him	Although Jesus told the people to tell no one, they told many.

Miracle	Scripture	Where	To or for Whom	Why	Results
Restoring sight to blind Bartimaeus	Matt. 20:29–34 Mark 10:46–52 Luke 18:35–43	Jericho	Bartimaeus	Bartimaeus's faith	Jesus' miracle was proclaimed by Bartimaeus and others.
Healing Syro-phoenician girl	Matt. 15:21–28 Mark 7:24–30	District of Tyre	Gentile woman of Syrophoenicia and her daughter	The woman's great faith	The girl was healed even though she was a Gentile.
Healing centurion's servant	Matt. 8:5–13 Luke 7:1–10	Capernaum	Centurion	To show what true faith is and that God's grace is open to all people, not just Israel	The man was healed.
Restoring demon-possessed man in synagogue	Mark 1:23–27 Luke 4:33–36	Capernaum	Jews	To rebuke the evil spirit	The evil spirit was cast out; people were amazed and the word spread to many.
Raising son of widow of Nain	Luke 7:11–16	Nain	Widow of Nain	Compassion	Jesus was hailed as a great prophet.
Restoring of woman crippled for eighteen years	Luke 13:10–17	At the house of one of the rulers of the Pharisees, somewhere between Galilee and Jerusalem	Sick woman	To cause discussion concerning healing on the Sabbath	Jesus' opponents were humiliated; His followers rejoiced.
Healing of man with dropsy	Luke 14:1–6	Jerusalem (?) or Perea (?)	Jews	To rebuke leaders about healing on the Sabbath	The officials could make no reply.
Healing of ten men with leprosy	Luke 17:11–19	On the road between Galilee and Jerusalem	Ten leprous men	To highlight the general rejection of Jesus by Israel and to show the responsibility concerning gratitude	Only one leper returned to thank Jesus.
Restoration of Malchus's ear	Luke 22:49–51 John 18:10–11	Garden of Gethsemane	Malchus, a servant of the high priest	In order to keep down tension in view of Peter's use of the sword.	

PART IV
The Apostolic Age

Major Events in New Testament History in the First Century A.D.

	Roman	Jewish	Christian
B.C.	Reign of Augustus as emperor (27 B.C.–A.D. 14) First census ordered by Quirinius, governor of Syria (6)	Reign of Herod the Great (37–4 B.C.) Beginning of Herod's temple (20 B.C.)	Birth of Jesus Christ (ca. 6–4)
A.D. 10	Reign of Tiberius (14–37)	Death of Herod the Great (4) Anointing of Caiaphas as high priest (18)	
20	Appointment of Pilate as prefect over Judea (26)		
30	Dismissal of Pilate by Rome (36) Reign of Caligula (37–41)	Reign of Herod Agrippa I (37–44)	John the Baptist's ministry (ca. 28–29) Beginning of Jesus' ministry (ca. 26–29) Crucifixion of Christ (c. 30–33) Pentecost (c. 30–33) Martyrdom of Stephen (c. 32 or 35) Conversion of Paul (c. 32–35)

Year	Roman	Jewish	Christian
40	Reign of Claudius (41–54)	Death of Herod Agrippa I (44) Expelling of Jews from Rome (49)	Martyrdom of James and imprisonment of Peter (between 41 and 44) Judean famine and Paul's relief visit (46–47) Paul's first missionary journey (47 or 48) Jerusalem Council (49) Paul's second missionary journey (49–51)
50	Reign of Nero (54–68)	Appointment of Felix as procurator (52–59) Appointment of Festus as procurator (59–61)	Paul's third missionary journey (52–57) Paul's arrest (57) Paul before Festus and Agrippa II; his appeal to Caesar (59)
60	Great fire of Rome; Christians blamed and persecuted (64–68) Reign of Vespasian (69–79)	Jewish revolt against Rome (66) Flight of Jerusalem Christians to Pella, east of Jordan (66)	Paul in Rome (60–61) Martyrdom of James, the Lord's brother (62) Martyrdom of Paul and Peter (between 64 and 68)
70		Fall of Jerusalem (70)	
	Reign of Titus (79–81)	Fall of Masada (73)	
80	Reign of Domitian (81–96)		
90			Roman persecution of church (94–96) Banishment of John the beloved to Patmos (94–96) Death of John (c. 100)

The *Kerygma* of the Early Church

1. The promises by God made in the Old Testament have now been fulfilled with the coming of Jesus the Messiah (Acts 2:30; 3:19, 24; 10:43; 26:6–7, 22; Rom. 1:2–4; 1 Tim. 3:16; Heb. 1:1–2; 1 Peter 1:10–12; 2 Peter 1:18–19).

2. Jesus was anointed by God at His baptism as Messiah (Acts 10:38).

3. Jesus began His ministry in Galilee after His baptism (Acts 10:37).

4. He conducted a beneficient ministry, doing good and performing mighty works by the power of God (Mark 10:45; Acts 2:22; 10:38).

5. The Messiah was crucified according to the purpose of God (Mark 10:45; John 3:16; Acts 2:23; 3:13–15, 18; 4:11; 10:39; 26:23; Rom. 8:34; 1 Cor. 1:17–18; 15:3; Gal. 1:4; Heb. 1:3; 1 Peter 1:2, 19; 3:18; 1 John 4:10).

6. He was raised from the dead and appeared to His disciples (Acts 2:24, 31–32; 3:15, 26; 10:40–41; 17:31; 26:23; Rom. 8:34; 10:9; 1 Cor. 15:4–7, 12ff.; 1 Thess. 1:10; 1 Tim. 3:16; 1 Peter 1:2, 21; 3:18, 21).

7. Jesus was exalted by God and given the name "Lord" (Acts 2:25–29, 33–36; 3:13; 10:36; Rom. 8:34; 10:9; 1 Tim. 3:16; Heb. 1:3; 1 Peter 3:22).

8. He gave the Holy Spirit to form the new community of God (Acts 1:8; 2:14–18, 33, 38–39; 10:44–47; 1 Peter 1:12).

9. He will come again for judgment and the restoration of all things (Acts 3:20–21; 10:42; 17:31; 1 Cor. 15:20–28; 1 Thess. 1:10).

10. All who hear the message should repent and be baptized (Acts 2:21, 38; 3:19; 10:43, 47–48; 17:30; 26:20; Rom. 1:17; 10:9; 1 Peter 3:21).

This schema served as the essential proclamation of the early church, though different authors of the New Testament may leave out a portion or vary in emphasis on particulars in the *kerygma*. Compare the entire gospel of Mark, which closely follows the Petrine aspect of the *kerygma*.

Possible Sources behind the Book of Acts

Type	Source	Comment
Eyewitness	Luke	In three sections of Acts (16:10–17; 20:5–15:18; 21:1–18; 27:1–28:16) the author changes his style from the third person ("he," "him," "they," "them") to the first person plural ("we," "our," "us"). These "we" passages give the impression that the author was present and participated in the events that he described. It may be that in these passages, highly detailed, Luke used notes he had kept in a diary. If this is true, the "we" sections depend on written material drawn from an eyewitness account.
Written	Apostolic decrees from Jerusalem	A copy of the decrees from the Jerusalem council may have been stored at Antioch (Acts 21:25) and may have been available to Luke.
Written	Jerusalem archives	The Jerusalem church may have had archives that Luke could have consulted.
Oral	Manaen	While he lived at Antioch, Luke may have gleaned information from Manaen concerning the Herodian dynasty. Manaen, an Antiochian Christian, was a member of the court of Herod the tetrarch (Acts 13:1). This may account for the fact that Luke is more detailed concerning the Herodian family than the other gospels.
Oral	Paul	The intimate knowledge that Luke had of Paul, being a traveling companion, would have allowed him to have discovered information about the earlier life and work of Paul.
Oral	Philip the evangelist	When Luke was at Caesarea, he stayed in the home of Philip the evangelist (Acts 21:8), from whom he might have acquired data about the appointment of the Seven (Acts 6:1–6), and Philip's experience with the Ethiopian official in the desert (Acts 8:26–40).
Oral	Mnason of Cyprus	Acts 21:16 states that Luke stayed with Mnason of Cyprus, from whom he could have learned about the church in Cyprus, which, as far as is known, he never visited.
Oral	James, the Lord's brother	When Luke was in Jerusalem, he had ample opportunity to visit with James, from whom he could have learned about the apostolic council (Acts 15:1–29) and other important events in the Jerusalem church.
Oral	Timothy, Silas, and other early church leaders	The remarks of Paul at the close of several of his letters (e.g., Col. and Philem.) indicate that Silas and Timothy were with Paul when Luke was present. From these two, as well as other early church leaders, Luke could have acquired needed information.

Luke's Presentation in Acts of the Growth of Christianity

Part	Panel	Scripture Portion	Content	Summary Statement
Introduction	–	1:1–2:41	The Constitutive Events of the Christian Mission	–
Part 1—The Christian Mission to the Jewish World	One	2:42–6:7	The Earliest Days of the Church at Jerusalem	6:7 ("So the word of God spread. The number of disciples in Jerusalem increased rapidly, and a large number of priests became obedient to the faith.")
	Two	6:8–9:31	Critical Events in the Lives of Three Pivotal Figures	9:31 ("Then the church throughout Judea, Galilee and Samaria enjoyed a time of peace. It was strengthened; and encouraged by the Holy Spirit, it grew in numbers, living in the fear of the Lord.")
	Three	9:32–12:24	Advances of the Gospel in Palestine-Syria	12:24 ("But the word of God continued to increase and spread.")
	Four	12:25–16:5	The First Missionary Journey and the Jerusalem Council	16:5 ("So the churches were strengthened in the faith and grew daily in numbers.")
Part 2—The Christian Mission to the Gentile World	Five	16:6–19:20	Wide Outreach through Two Missionary Journeys	19:20 ("In this way the word of the Lord spread widely and grew in power.")
	Six	19:21–28:31	To Jerusalem and Thence to Rome	28:30–31 ("Boldly and without hindrance he preached the kingdom of God and taught about the Lord Jesus Christ.")

Adapted from Richard N. Longenecker, "Acts," in *The Expositor's Bible Commentary: With the New International Version of the Holy Bible*, vol. 9, ed. Frank Gaebelein (Grand Rapids: Zondervan, 1984). [CD-ROM].

123

Parallels between the Structures of Luke and Acts

Parallel	Scripture Portion	Luke Content	Scripture Portion	Acts Content
Introductory Section	1:1–2:52	Luke begins with an introductory section, dealing with Jesus' birth and youth before taking up the narrative of Jesus' ministry.	1:1–2:41	Acts begins with an introductory section dealing with the constitutive events of the Christian mission before it sets forth the advances of the gospel "in Jerusalem, and in all Judea and Samaria, and to the ends of the earth" (1:7).
Thematic Paragraph	4:14–30	The Nazareth pericope serves as the topical paragraph for all that Luke presents in his two volumes; most of what follows is an explication of the themes it contains.	2:42–47	Introductory section is followed by what appears to be a thematic statement (2:42–47). This material most probably serves as the thesis paragraph for what follows.
Geographical Outline	4:14–24:53	Luke follows an essentially geographical outline that moves from the Galilean ministry (4:14–9:50), through Perea and Judea (9:51-19:28), and concludes in Jerusalem (19:29-24:53)	2:42–28:31	Luke follows an essentially geographical outline that moves from Jerusalem (2:42–6:7), through Judea and Samaria (6:8–9:31), on into Palestine-Syria (9:32–12:24), then to the Gentiles in the eastern part of the Roman Empire (12:25–19:20), and finally culminates in Paul's defenses and the entrance of the gospel into Rome (19:21–28:31).
Literary Parallels	–	Luke sets up a number of parallels between Jesus' ministry in Galilee and His ministry in the regions of Perea and Judea.	–	Luke sets up a number of parallels between the ministry of Peter in the first half of Acts and that of Paul in the last half.

Adapted from Richard N. Longenecker, "Acts," in *The Expositor's Bible Commentary: With the New International Version of the Holy Bible*, vol. 9, ed. Frank Gaebelein (Grand Rapids: Zondervan, 1984). [CD-ROM].

Paul's Missionary Journeys

Place	Date	Acts	Significant Events
First Missionary Journey			
Cyprus	47–48	13:1–12	False prophet, Bar-Jesus, blinded; proconsul Sergius Paulus converted; Saul called Paul
Perga in Pamphylia	48–49	13:13	John Mark returned home
Pisidian Antioch		13:14–52	Paul and Barnabas preached to Jews and Gentiles in synagogue; Jews stirred up persecution against Paul and Barnabas and expelled them from region
Iconium		14:1–5	A great number of Jews and Gentiles believed; unbelieving Jews caused division in city
Lystra		14:6–20	Barnabas identified as Zeus; Paul, as Hermes; Paul stoned
Derbe		14:20–21	A large number of disciples won
Lystra		14:21–23	Strengthening and encouraging of disciples and appointing of elders
Pisidian Antioch Pamphylia Perga Attalia		14:24–25	To Pamphylia, Perga, and Attalia
Antioch		14:26–28	Report of how gospel was accepted by Gentiles
Apostolic Council in Jerusalem			
Antioch	49	15:1–2	Paul and Barnabas in sharp dispute with Judaizers from Judea
Phoenicia		15:3	Report of how Gentiles were converted; people rejoiced
Samaria		15:3	Welcomed by church
Jerusalem		15:4–6	Question of God's acceptance of Gentiles; speeches by Peter, Paul, Barnabas, and James
		15:7–21	
		15:22–29	Problem resolved; Paul, Barnabas, Judas, and Silas sent with letter
		15:30–35	Letter received; people encouraged and strengthened; Paul and Barnabas remain and teach

Second Missionary Journey

Place	Date	Acts	Significant Events
Antioch	49–51	15:36–40	Beginning of journey; Paul and Barnabas disagreed over taking John Mark; Barnabas took John Mark
	50–52		Paul took Silas
Syria and Cilicia		15:41	
Derbe		16:1	Timothy joined them
Lystra		16:1–5	
Iconium		16:1–5	
Phrygia and Galatia		16:6–7	
Troas		16:8–9	Paul's vision to go to Macedonia; Luke began using first person in v. 10
Philippi		16:10–40	Lydia converted; demon-possessed fortune-teller delivered; Paul and Silas jailed; earthquake; jailer converted
Thessalonica		17:1–9	Jews, Greeks, and women believed; jealous Jews caused turmoil, mobbed Jason's house
Berea		17:10–14	Jews, Greek men and women believed; Jews from Thessalonica came and stirred up people
Athens		17:15–34	Paul preached about "Unknown God"; a few believed
Corinth	52	18:1–17	Crispus converted; Paul's vision to stay; many Corinthians believed and were baptized; met Aquila and Priscilla; Sosthenes beaten
Ephesus		18:18–21	Asked to stay and preach, but declined; left Aquila and Priscilla
Caesarea		18:22	
Antioch		18:22–23	

Third Missionary Journey

Place	Date	Acts	Significant Events
Antioch	52–56	18:23	Beginning of journey
Galatia and Phrygia	53–56	18:23	Disciples strengthened
Ephesus		18:24–19:41	Miracles; Word of the Lord spreads widely and grows in power; riot of silversmiths
Macedonia and Greece		20:1–6	Plot to kill Paul on voyage
Troas		20:7–12	Eutychus fell from window; Paul brought him back to life
Miletus		20:13–38	Paul's farewell to Ephesian elders; encouragement
To Jerusalem		21:1–16	Agabus warned Paul of what would happen in Jerusalem
Jerusalem		21:17–26	Paul reported what God had done among the Gentiles; Paul took a Jewish vow

Paul's Arrest and Imprisonment

Situation	Date	Acts	Significant Events
Paul arrested	56	21:27–36	City mob; soldiers arrested Paul
Paul speaks	57	21:37–22:22	Paul defended himself; gave testimony; crowd angered again
Paul—Roman citizen		22:23–29	Because of angry crowd, Paul to be flogged; commander alarmed when he found that Paul was a Roman citizen
Paul before Sanhedrin		22:30–23:11	Paul testified and Pharisees and Sadducees disputed
Plot to kill Paul		23:12–22	Son of Paul's sister warned commander
Paul's escape		23:23–30	Detachment, Paul, and letter travel to Governor Felix at Caesarea
At Caesarea	57–59	23:31–25:12	Paul on trial before Felix and Festus
Paul and Agrippa		25:13–26	Agrippa told Festus that Paul could have been set free if he had not appealed to Caesar
Paul sails for Rome		27:1–12	Voyage began; Paul's advice not to sail rejected
The storm		27:13–26	Paul urged courage; told of angel's message and faith in God
The shipwreck		27:27–44	Paul encouraged others; ship ran aground; everyone reached land safely
Malta	60–61	28:1–10	Paul not killed by snake; healed man
Rome	60–61	28:11–31	Paul preached salvation unhindered

A Chronology of the Apostolic Age

Event	Date
The outpouring of the Spirit at Pentecost (Acts 2:1ff.)	A.D. 30
The stoning of Stephen (Acts 7:1ff.)	32 or 33
Paul's conversion to Christianity (Acts 9:1ff.)	32–35
Paul's silent years	35–43
Paul's trip to Antioch	43
James (epistle of) written	c. 45
Paul's first missionary journey (Acts 13–14)	47 or 48
Peter at Antioch (Gal. 2:11–16)	late 48 or early 49
Galatians written	late 48 or early 49
The apostolic council at Jerusalem (Acts 15:1–35)	49
Paul's second missionary journey (Acts 15:36–18:22)	49–51
1 and 2 Thessalonians written	50 or 51
Paul's third missionary journey (Acts 18:23–21:16) (some date Paul's captivity letters during his stay in Ephesus)	52–56
1 and 2 Corinthians written	54 and 56
Romans written	55 or 56
Paul's arrest (Acts 21:26–23)	56
Paul's appearance before Felix and Drusilla (Acts 24:24–26)	57
Paul's imprisonment in Caesarea (Acts 24:27) (some put Paul's captivity letters here)	57–59
Paul's trial before Festus (Acts 25:7–12)	59
Paul's trial before Agrippa (Acts 26)	59
The voyage to Rome (Acts 27:1–28:29)	59 or 60
Paul's first Roman imprisonment (Acts 28:30)	60 or 62
Philemon written	60 or 61
Colossians written	60 or 61

Event	Date
Ephesians written	60 or 61
Luke written	60 or 61
Acts written	61 or 62
Philippians written	61 or 62
Paul's release	62
Paul's possible trip to Spain (Rom. 15:24–28)	62
The martyrdom of James, the Lord's brother	62
Peter in Rome	62
Mark written	late 50s or early 60s
Paul in Macedonia	63–67
1 Timothy written	63–67
Paul's trip to Crete	63–67
Titus written	63–67
1 Peter written	63–67
Paul taken to Rome	63–67
2 Timothy written	63–67
2 Peter written	63–67
Paul's second Roman imprisonment and subsequent death	63–67
Peter's death	63–67
Matthew written	60s
Hebrews written	60s
The destruction of Jerusalem	70
Jude written	60s or 70s
John written	late 80s or early 90s
1, 2, 3 John written	late 80s or early 90s
Revelation written	mid-90s
1 Clement written	92–101
John's death at Ephesus	c. 98–100

An Alternate Chronology

Crucifixion	Friday, April 3, 33
Pentecost (Acts 2)	Sunday, May 24, 33
Peter's second sermon; Peter brought before Sanhedrin (Acts 3:1–4:31)	summer 33
Death of Ananias and Sapphira (Acts 4:32–5:11)	33–34
Peter brought before Sanhedrin (Acts 5:12–42)	34–35
Deacons selected (Acts 6:1–7)	late 34–early 35
Stephen martyred (Acts 6:8–7:60)	April 35
Paul's conversion (Acts 9:1–7)	summer 35
Paul in Damascus and Arabia (Acts 9:8–25; Gal. 1:16–17)	summer 35–early summer 37
Paul in Jerusalem, first visit (Acts 9:26–29; Gal. 1:18–20)	summer 37
Paul to Tarsus and Syria-Cilicia area (Acts 9:30; Gal. 1:21)	autumn 37
Peter's ministry to Gentiles (Acts 10:1–11:18)	40–41
Barnabas to Antioch (Acts 11:19–24)	41
Paul to Antioch (Acts 11:25–26)	spring 43
Agabus's prediction of famine (Acts 11:27–28)	spring 44
Agrippa's persecution, James martyred (Acts 12:1–23)	spring 44
Relief visit, Paul's second visit to Jerusalem (Acts 11:30; Gal. 2:1–10)	autumn 47
Paul in Antioch (Acts 12:25–13:1)	autumn 47–spring 48
First missionary journey (Acts 13–14)	April 48–Sept. 49
Departure from Antioch	April 48
Cyprus	April–June 48
Pamphylia	first of July–middle of July 48
Pisidian Antioch	middle of July–middle of Sept. 48
Iconium	Oct. 48–last of Feb. 49
Lystra-Derbe	March–middle of June 49
Return visit to churches	middle of June–Aug. 49
Return to Antioch of Syria	Sept. 49
Peter in Antioch (Gal. 2:11–16)	autumn 49
Galatians written from Antioch	autumn 49

Jerusalem council, Paul's third visit (Acts 15)	autumn 49
Paul in Antioch (Acts 12:25–13:1)	winter 49/50
Second missionary journey (Acts 15:35–18:22)	April 50–Sept. 52
Departure from Antioch	April 50
Syria and Cilicia	April 50
Lystra-Derbe	May 50
Iconium	last of May–middle of June 50
Pisidian Antioch	middle of June–first of July 50
Antioch to Troas	July 50
Philippi	Aug.–Oct. 50
Thessalonica	Nov. 50–Jan. 51
Berea	Feb. 51
Athens	last of Feb.–middle of March 51
Arrival at Corinth	middle of March 51
Silas and Timothy arrive from Berea	April/May 51
1 Thessalonians written	early summer 51
2 Thessalonians written	summer 51
Departure from Corinth	first of Sept. 52
Ephesus	middle of Sept. 52
Jerusalem, Paul's fourth visit	last of Sept. 52
Return to Antioch	first/middle of Nov. 52
Paul's stay at Antioch	winter 52/53
Third missionary journey (Acts 18:23–21:16)	spring 53–May 57
Departure from Antioch	spring 53
Visiting Galatian churches	spring–summer 53
Arrival at Ephesus	Sept. 53
1 Corinthians written	early spring 56
Departure from Ephesus (riot)	first of May 56
Troas	May 56
Arrival in Macedonia	first of June 56
2 Corinthians written	Sept./Oct. 56
Departure from Macedonia	middle of Nov. 56
Arrival in Corinth	last of Nov. 56
Romans written	winter 56/57

Departure from Corinth	last of Feb. 57
Philippi	April 6–14, 57
Troas	April 19–25, 57
Troas to Assos	Monday, April 25, 57
Assos to Mitylene	April 26, 57
Mitylene to Chios	April 27, 57
Chios to Trogyllium	April 28, 57
Trogyllium to Miletus	April 29, 57
Ephesian elders' visit with Paul	April 30–May 2
Miletus to Patara	May 2–4, 57
Patara to Tyre	May 5–9, 57
Stay at Tyre	May 10–16, 57
Tyre to Caesarea	May 17–19, 57
Stay at Caesarea	May 19–25, 57
Caesarea to Jerusalem	May 25–27, 57
Jerusalem, Paul's fifth visit	eve of Pentecost, May 27, 57
Meeting with James (Acts 21:13–23)	May 28, 57
Paul's arrest and trial before Felix (Acts 21:26–24:22)	May 29–June 9, 57
First day of purification	Sunday, May 29, 57
Second day of purification	May 30, 57
Third day of purification	May 31, 57
Fourth day of purification	June 1, 57
Fifth day of purification, riot, Paul's speech	June 2, 57
Paul before the Sanhedrin	June 3, 57
Appearance of the Lord (night)	
Conspiracy (day)	June 4, 57
Journey to Antipatris (night)	
Journey to Caesarea (day)	June 5, 57
Waiting in Caesarea for trial	June 5–9, 57
Trial before Felix	Thursday, June 9, 57
Paul before Felix and Drusilla (Acts 24:24–26)	June 57
Caesarean imprisonment (Acts 24:27)	June 57–Aug. 59
Trial before Festus (Acts 25:7–12)	July 59
Trial before Agrippa (Acts 26)	first of Aug. 59

Voyage to Rome (Acts 27:1–28:29)	Aug. 59–Feb. 60
Departure from Caesarea	middle of Aug. 59
Myra	first of Sept. 59
Fair Havens	Oct. 5–10, 59
Shipwreck at Malta	last of Oct. 59
Departure from Malta	first of Feb. 60
Arrival in Rome	last of Feb. 60
First Roman imprisonment (Acts 28:30)	Feb. 60–March 62
Ephesians written	autumn 60
Colossians and Philemon written	autumn 61
Philippians written	early spring 62
James, the Lord's brother, martyred	spring 62
Paul in Ephesus and Colosse	spring–autumn 62
Peter went to Rome	62
Paul in Macedonia	late summer 62–winter 62/63
1 Timothy written	autumn 62
Paul in Asia Minor	spring 63–spring 64
Paul in Spain	spring 64–spring 66
Christians persecuted, Peter martyred	summer 64
Paul in Crete	early summer 66
Paul in Asia Minor	summer–autumn 66
Titus written	summer 66
Paul in Nicopolis	winter 66/67
Paul in Macedonia and Greece	spring–autumn 67
Paul arrested and brought to Rome	autumn 67
2 Timothy written	autumn 67
Paul's death	spring 68
Destruction of Jerusalem	Sept. 2, 70

Adapted from Harold Hoehner, "A Chronological Table of the Apostolic Age" (a handout by the author, April 1972), by permission.

The Twelve Apostles

Facts	Scriptures
First Group	
Peter: given name Simon, changed to Cephas (Aramaic) or Peter (Greek); native of Bethsaida; son of John, brother of Andrew; fisherman, home in Capernaum; present at transfiguration and Gethsemane; denied Christ; first apostle to (1) preach the gospel, (2) perform a miracle, (3) speak before the Sanhedrin, (4) preach to Gentiles, (5) raise the dead; traditionally martyred at Rome in A.D. 67	Too extensive to list, but note Gal. 2:7–9; 1, 2 Peter
Andrew: introduced brother Peter to Jesus; son of John; native of Bethsaida; fisherman; traditionally martyred in Greece; brought word to Jesus of Greeks who wanted to see Him	Matt. 4:18; 10:2; Mark 1:16, 29; 3:18; 13:3; Luke 6:14; John 1:40, 44; 6:8; 12:22; Acts 1:13
James: brother of John; son of Zebedee and Salome; fisherman, with father and brother partners with Peter; present at transfiguration and in Gethsemane; called by Jesus a "Son of Thunder"; martyred by Herod Agrippa I (c. A.D. 44)	Matt. 4:21; 10:2; 17:1; Mark 1:19, 29; 3:17; 5:37; 9:2; 10:35, 41; 13:3; 14:33; Luke 5:10; 6:14; 8:51; 9:28, 54; Acts 1:13; 12:2
John: brother of James; son of Zebedee and Salome; fisherman, partner with Peter; present at transfiguration and in Gethsemane; called by Jesus "Son of Thunder"; "the disciple whom Jesus loved"; companion of Peter; cared for Mary, the Lord's mother; leader in Jerusalem church; later moved to Ephesus; exiled to isle of Patmos; traditionally not martyred	Matt. 4:21; 10:2; 17:1; Mark 1:19, 29; 3:17; 5:37; 9:2, 38; 10:35, 41; 13:3; 14:33; Luke 5:10; 6:14; 8:51; 9:28, 49, 54; 22:8; Acts 1:13; 3:1, 3–4, 11; 4:13, 19; 8:14; 12:2; Gal. 2:9; Rev. 1:1, 4, 9; 22:8. Cf. 1, 2, 3 John, gospel of John

Adapted from Merland Ray Miller, "Timetables and Charts for the New Testament," ThM thesis (Portland, Ore.: Western Conservative Baptist Seminary, 1980), by permission.

Facts	Scriptures
Second Group	
Philip: native of Bethsaida; told Nathanael of Jesus; brought word to Jesus of Greeks who wanted to see Him; traditions unclear	Matt. 10:3; Mark 3:18; Luke 6:14; John 1:43–46, 48; 6:5, 7; 12:21–22; 14:8–9; Acts 1:13
Bartholomew: probably Nathanael of John's gospel; from Cana; name Bartholomew Aramaic for "Son of Tolmai"; Jesus saw him under the fig tree; traditionally martyred in Armenia	Matt. 10:3; Mark 3:18; Luke 6:14; John 1:45–49; 21:2; Acts 1:13
Thomas (called Didymus): probably from Galilee; claimed he was willing to die with Jesus; asked Jesus how to know the way; doubted Jesus' resurrection; traditionally preached in India	Matt. 10:3; Mark 3:18; Luke 6:15; John 11:16; 14:5; 20:24, 26–28; 21:2; Acts 1:13
Matthew: tax collector; son of Alphaeus; also known as Levi; held a great feast for Jesus in his house; tradition unclear	Matt. 9:9; 10:3; Mark 2:14; 3:18; Luke 5:27, 29; 6:15; Acts 1:13
Third Group	
James: son of Alphaeus and Mary; known as "the small" or "the Younger"; brother of Joseph; tradition unclear due to confusion with other Jameses	Matt. 10:3; 27:56; Mark 3:18; 15:40; 16:1; Luke 6:15; 24:10; Acts 1:13
Judas (not Iscariot): son of James; also called Thaddaeus; perhaps a Zealot; traditionally preached in Armenia and martyred in Persia with Simon the Zealot	Matt. 10:3; Mark 3:18; Luke 6:16; John 14:22; Acts 1:13
Simon the Zealot: traditionally martyred in Persia with Jude	Matt. 10:4; Mark 3:18; Luke 6:15; Acts 1:13
Judas Iscariot: possibly from Judea; betrayer of Christ; called by Jesus "devil" and "son of perdition"; treasurer for the apostolic band; committed suicide	Matt. 10:4; 26:14, 25, 47; 27:3, 5; Mark 3:19; 14:10, 43; Luke 6:16; 22:3, 47–48; John 6:71; 12:4; 13:2, 26, 29; 18:2–3, 5; Acts 1:16, 18, 25

Corinthian Correspondence and Visits

Event	Scripture Reference
Founding of church on second missionary journey	Acts 18:1–17
Leaving Corinth, arriving at Ephesus	Acts 18:18–19
Writing a letter now lost	1 Cor. 5:9–13
Receiving a bad report from "some from Chloe's household" and a letter from Corinth	1 Cor. 1:11; 7:1
Writing of 1 Corinthians	1 Corinthians
Sending of Timothy and Erastus to Corinth	Acts 19:22; 1 Cor. 4:17; 16:10
Hearing of serious crisis in Corinth caused by Jewish emissaries in which Paul's authority is questioned	2 Cor. 10:10; 11:23; 12:6–7
Making a hasty trip to Corinth ("painful visit")	2 Cor. 2:1; 12:14; 13:1
Writing of "severe letter" to Corinth	2 Cor. 2:3–9; 7:8–12
Searching for Titus in Troas and Macedonia	2 Cor. 2:12–13
Finding of Titus, who reports worst at Corinth is over	2 Cor. 7:6–16
Writing of 2 Corinthians	2 Corinthians
Making third visit to Corinth	Acts 19:21; 20:3; 2 Cor. 13:1

The Destination of the Letter to the Galatians

Introduction: The evidence that follows is used by scholars who are seeking to prove (1) whether Paul wrote Galatians to the churches that he and Barnabas started during the first missionary journey in the southern part of the Roman province of Galatia, or (2) whether Paul wrote Galatians to churches founded during the second and third missionary journeys, Galatia being understood in a territorial sense, the area founded by the Gauls, as it was before becoming Roman territory in 25 B.C.

Available evidence does not absolutely settle the issue, but older and more liberal commentators favor the North Galatia theory (2), while more recent and most evangelical commentators favor South Galatia (1), feeling that an earlier date for the book of Galatians and better explanation of the historical setting are compelling arguments.

Northern Galatia Theory

Evidence For	Evidence Against
1. Luke uses territorial, not Roman provincial, titles to describe the regions encompassed by Paul's itinerary (Acts 13:14; 14:6; 16:6; 18:23). Since he mentions, for example, Pisidia (Acts 13:14) and Lycaonia (Acts 14:6) in that way, it is reasonable that he uses territorial terminology when mentioning the apostle's journey through the Galatian region.	1. It is difficult to determine the real meaning of Luke's words. Literally he said that Paul went through the "Phrygian-Galatic country" (Acts 16:6) and later through "the Galatic-Phrygian country" (Acts 18:23), a designation that could refer to either the territory or province or both. Also, though Acts does contain references to Paul's work in North Galatia, it is unusual that such meager material is given about churches where such a controversy, as mentioned in Galatians, occurred.
2. Since there is no mention of Paul's physical infirmity during the first journey (Acts 13–14), why would Paul refer to it in the letter (Gal. 4:13)?	2. Luke does not mention Paul's infirmity in his accounts of the second or third journeys either. Many of Paul's persecutions and illnesses were not recorded by Luke or even by Paul himself (cf. 2 Cor. 11–12).
3. Paul would have referred to his persecutions, including the stoning episode, if he had written to the Southern Galatian churches.	3. Paul did mention the marks that his body bore for his faith and testimony (Gal. 6:17). It is conceivable that his eye problem (Gal. 4:13–15) was caused or aggravated by the stoning incident.

Evidence For	Evidence Against
4. This was the traditional view of the church until the eighteenth century.	4. In the second century A.D. the area of Lycaonia Galatia was detached from Galatia as it was originally and united to Cilicia to form an enlarged province. Toward the end of the third century the remainder of South Galatia became the province of Pisidia, with Pisidian Antioch as its capital city and Iconium as its second city. The province of Galatia was thus virtually reduced to the northern part of the area. So patristic writers read Galatians 1:2 in the sense familiar to them and considered "Galatia" to refer to the northern tracts of country as in their day. Such confusion of understanding existed during most of church history.
5. If the Epistle to the Galatians was sent to the churches founded on his first missionary journey, Paul would not have said, "Later I went to Syria and Cilicia" (1:21) but something like, "Then I went to Syria, Cilicia, and to you."	5. This supposed Pauline phraseology is simply speculative.
6. Paul could not possibly have addressed Lycaonians or Pisidians, "You foolish Galatians" (Gal. 3:1). Writers contemporary with Paul clearly distinguished the Galatians from their neighboring tribes.	6. If Lycaonia and Pisidia are rightfully part of Roman Galatia and if they truly departed from the apostle's teaching, then "You foolish Galatians," is quite appropriate for them and not simply reserved for the people of the Galatian region.
7. The original use of the term *Galatia* refers to the northern territory. This is analogous to other places such as Mysia, Phrygia, and Pisidia, all of which are geographical expressions lacking any political significance. These occur in the same parts of the narrative with Galatians; so the latter seemingly would be used in the same way.	7. That the term *Galatia* originally referred to northern Galatia is beside the point. Paul used the Roman provincial titles often.
8. Paul often mentions an area by its regional name rather than political name, and the *region* of Galatia was in the north; e.g., Rom. 15:31; 2 Cor. 1:16; Gal. 1:17, 21; 1 Thess. 2:14.	8. Paul, however, also used provincial names. In the context of provincial Macedonia (1 Cor. 16:5), Achaia (1 Cor. 16:15), and Asia (1 Cor. 16:19), he alludes to Galatia (1 Cor. 16:1), most likely as a provincial name.

Evidence For	Evidence Against
9. The people who settled northern Galatia moved to that area from a place far west. They were of Celtic origen but were designated as *Galate* by the Greeks and *Galli* by the Romans. The character of the people addressed in Paul's epistle is like that of these Galatians. They were a "fickle" race, in harmony with Paul's statement "you are changing so quickly." This is in agreement with the description found in Caesar and Cicero.	9. Hardly should those people in the region of Galatia be considered the only ones capable of being "fickle." This is highly questionable argumentation.

Southern Galatia Theory

Evidence For	Evidence Against
1. Acts contains territorial designations, whereas Paul chose to use provincial titles. In 1 Corinthians Paul alluded to the churches of Galatia (16:1); in that same context, he referred to other regions by their provincial names: Macedonia (16:5), Achaia (16:15), and Asia (16:19). Thus Paul most likely used "Galatia" as a provincial title also.	1. Paul often used territorial rather than official names, e.g., Syria (in Gal. 1:21) for Seleucidian Syria, in which was Antioch rather than the broader Roman province to which also Jerusalem belonged. In reference to Christians in Judea, he was thinking of the territory of Judea (2 Cor. 1:16; 1 Thess. 2:14); Arabia was territorial, not a name for the kingdom of the Nabatians (Gal. 1:17).
2. Paul, more likely, wrote to churches whose establishment is recorded in Acts (chs. 13–14) than to churches about which we have little information.	2. Also, little is known about the founding of the Colossian church.
3. The Judaizers, the enemies of Paul, would have invaded the densely populated area of southern Galatia, below the Taurus Mountains, where Jews and synagogues were located rather than the sparsely settled and inaccessible northern sections.	3. Nothing is known about these envoys from Jerusalem. They could have gone into the territory of Galatia without there being any knowledge of it.
4. The reference to Barnabas, especially his defection at Antioch (Gal. 2;1, 9; Cf. 2:13), would have significance only to the southern Galatians because Barnabas was with Paul during the first journey, but not during the next two.	4. In 1 Cor. 7:6 Paul refers to Barnabas as known in Corinth, and there is no evidence he had visited that church.

Evidence For	Evidence Against
5. Since there is no reference to the historic decision made at the council of Jerusalem (Acts 15), a decision that would have provided Paul with a clinching argument, the book must have been written before that event occurred. In that case Paul could have written only to the Southern Galatian churches of Antioch, Iconium, Lystra, and Derbe.	5. The reference to the council does not occur in any of Paul's letters, even at points on Jew-Gentile relations and the gospel. Also, it may be that Paul did not consider the council's decision a real or final victory for him and the gospel.
6. Although Peter was an unstable person at times, his defection at Antioch (2:11–14) would better fit into his life experiences before the council at Jerusalem than after.	6. Why should the decision of the council be more compelling against a defection than the testimony of the Holy Spirit at Cornelius's house a few years before?
7. There were Jews in the churches of the province of Galatia, but almost nothing is known of Jews in the territory of Galatia. So it is more likely that Paul would have gone to the Jewish groups of southern Galatia.	7. The references in Galatians that could refer to Jewish Christians (3:2–3, 13–14, 23–24; 4:2, 5; 5:1) are general statements to Christians. The Galatians were Gentile Christians (4:8; 5:2–3; 6:12–13).
8. According to Acts 20:4, Paul had Christians from the province of Galatia (Gaius of Derbe and Timothy of Lystra) assist with the collection, but none were from the territory of Galatia, though according to 1 Corinthians 16:1 the collection was gathered in Galatia.	8. Acts 20:4 also mentions no bearers from Achaia, though they would be expected, according to 1 Corinthians 16:1. Also, Gaius may have been a Macedonian (Acts 19:29; 20:4, Codex D[?]).
9. The epistle to the Galatians implies that the apostle founded the Galatian church due to an interrupted transit through their country. Since southern Galatia was heavily traveled, having a major highway, whereas northern Galatia was far from the normal travel routes, the only possible reason to visit northern Galatia would be for the conversion of the people. Southern Galatia better squares with the circumstances of the founding of the church in Galatia.	9. The desire to go into Galatia "merely" for conversion is well within Pauline strategy. Note his desire to go into Bythinia, an area also out of the way. Also, who may know the apostle's inward motivations?

Similarities between Ephesians and Colossians

Similarity[1]	Ephesians	Colossians
Origin	Assuming Pauline authorship, letter was written from prison to the churches of Ephesus	Written by Paul from prison
Writing Style	Both books contain long sentences and numerous relative clauses, genitive constructions, and prepositional phrases	
Vocabulary	26.5 percent of the 2,411 words in Ephesians are paralleled in Colossians	34 percent of the 1,570 words in Colossians are paralleled in Ephesians
Extended Parallels	1:1–2	1:1–2
	3:2	1:25
	3:9	1:26
	1:7	1:14
	4:16	2:19
Similar Subject Matter[2]		
Prescript	1:1–2	1:1–2
Thanksgiving/Intercessory prayer	1:3–14	1:3–14
Transformation from alienation to reconciliation	2:11–22	1:21–23
Paul as suffering apostle and his ministry of the mystery	3:1–13	1:24–29
Head-body relation	4:15–16	2:19
Old and new humanity	4:17–5:20	3:5–17
Household code	5:21–6:9	3:18–4:1
Exhortation to prayer	4:2–4	6:18–20
Commendation of Tychicus	4:7–9	6:21–22

[1] This chart is derived from Andrew T. Lincoln, *Ephesians*, WBC, vol. 42 (Dallas: Word Books, 1990). [CD-ROM].

[2] For a similar list of topical parallels, see Raymond E. Brown, *An Introduction to the New Testament* (New York: Doubleday, 1997), 628.

Arguments concerning the Pauline Authorship of Ephesians

Arguments For	Arguments Against
1. Wide circulation in the early church; placed within the earliest formal canon of the NT (Marcion's) and later in the Muratorian Canon; possible references to Ephesians in early Christian documents (Clement of Rome, Hermas, Barnabas, Ignatius, Tertullian, Clement of Alexandria, and Origen)	1. Common words in Ephesians and Colossians bear different meanings (e.g., "mystery" in Ephesians is applied to Christ, whereas Colossians uses "mystery" in the context of Jew-Gentile unification)
2. Ephesians claims to have been written by Paul (Eph. 1:1; 3:1); other personal references fit Paul's life	2. Ephesians differs from Paul's other letters since no concrete situation is under discussion in the letter
3. Typical Pauline literary structure (salutation, thanksgiving, doctrinal exposition, moral appeal, final courtesies, and benediction)	3. Complex writing style and sentence structures (unlike other Pauline writings)
4. Unique words and phrases in Ephesians are similar in number to Galatians, an undisputed Pauline letter	4. Almost one hundred words and phrases not found elsewhere in Paul
5. Lack of personal references can be explained by the encyclical nature of the letter; Paul kept his references general for a varied audience	5. Lack of personal references (considered an unlikely circumstance if Paul, who ministered in Ephesus for 3 years, wrote Ephesians)
6. Literary correspondence between Ephesians and Colossians, a letter most consider Pauline	6. Similarity with Colossians; Ephesians is considered by some to be a generalized version of Colossians
7. Broad similarities in language with the rest of the Pauline corpus	7. Dependence of Ephesians on other Pauline letters for content
8. Although new theological themes appear, the basic theological emphases are consistent with other Pauline letters	8. Different theology from other Pauline writings (universal church, apostolic authority, cosmic Christology)
9. Several historical features indicate an early date (no mention of the destruction of the Temple, absence of persecution, absence of developed ecclesiology)	9. Pauline concerns from the undisputed letters (e.g., the return of Christ, the issues of circumcision and the Law, and justification) are less acute in Ephesians
Advocates	**Advocates**
O'Brien, Bruce, C. H. Dodd, Guthrie	F. C. Baur, Käsemann, Conzelmann, Raymond Brown, Goodspeed, Lincoln, Holtzmann, Mitton

Sources Consulted:

Brown, Raymond E. *An Introduction to the New Testament.* New York: Doubleday, 1997.

Guthrie, Donald. *New Testament Introduction.* 4th rev. ed. Downers Grove, Ill.: InterVarsity, 1990.

Lincoln, Andrew T. *Ephesians.* Word Biblical Commentary. Vol. 42. Dallas: Word Books, 1990. [CD-ROM].

Wood, A. Skevington. "Ephesians." In *The Expositor's Bible Commentary: With the New International Version of the Holy Bible.* Vol. 11. Edited by Frank Gaebelein. Grand Rapids: Zondervan, 1978.

Arguments concerning the Pauline Authorship of Colossians

Arguments For	Arguments Against
1. Colossians claims to have been written by Paul (Col. 1:1, 23; 4:18)	1. Redundant literary style atypical of Paul
2. Unique words and phrases in Colossians are similar in number to Philippians, an undisputed Pauline letter	2 Approximately 90 words in Colossians are not found elsewhere in Paul
3. Unique words and phrases may be accounted for by the heresy Paul combats in Colossians	3. Absence of Pauline terms such as "justification," "believe," and "law"
4. Dating the various controversies is highly speculative work; incipient Gnosticism was certainly possible	4. Gnostic heresy under discussion represents later church concerns, not the problems of the middle first century
5. Paul elsewhere considers Christ identified with the body, the church (1 Cor. 1:13; 12:12)	5. Developed ecclesiology; Christ is considered the head of the body, the church (1:18); the church is considered local (4:15–16) and universal (1:18, 24)
6. Cosmic Christology is evident in other Pauline writings (Rom. 8:19–22; 1 Cor. 8:6)	6. Cosmic Christology represents later development in Christian theology
7. Although realized eschatology is present in a sense, future eschatology is also apparent (3:4, 6, 24); the balance between the two is typically Pauline	7. Realized eschatology apparent in Colossians (1:26–27; 3:1–4)
8. Close link with Philemon (Col. 1:1// Phm. 1; Col. 4:10–14//Phm. 23–24; Col. 4:9//Phm. 10), an undisputed letter of Paul, argues for Pauline authorship	
9. No evidence that Pauline authorship was questioned until the 19th century	
10. Placed within the earliest formal canon of the NT (Marcion's) and later in the Muratorian Canon	
11. Irenaeus, Clement of Alexandria, and Origen all quoted the letter as Pauline	
Advocates	**Advocates**
Bruce, Kümmel, O'Brien	Baur, Holtzmann, Conzelmann, Marxsen

Sources Consulted:

Brown, Raymond E. *An Introduction to the New Testament.* New York: Doubleday, 1997.

Guthrie, Donald. *New Testament Introduction.* 4th rev. ed. Downers Grove, Ill.: InterVarsity, 1990.

O'Brien, Peter T. *Colossians, Philemon.* Word Biblical Commentary. Vol. 44. Dallas: Word Books, 1982. [CD-ROM].

Vaughan, Curtis. "Colossians." In *The Expositor's Bible Commentary: With the New International Version of the Holy Bible.* Vol. 11. Edited by Frank Gaebelein. Grand Rapids: Zondervan, 1978.

| Arguments concerning the Pauline Authorship of 2 Thessalonians ||
Arguments For	Arguments Against
1. 2 Thessalonians claims to have been written by Paul (1:1; 3:17)	1. Greater use of the OT, indicating a Jewish rather than Gentile audience (in contrast to 1 Thessalonians)
2. Need for validation of the letter (3:17) may be accounted for by the circulation of inauthentic letters (2:12)	2. In Paul's day there was no need to guarantee the authenticity of his letters
3. Writer gives evidence of intimate knowledge of the Thessalonian situation (3:6–15)	3. Emphasis on relief for the persecuted rather than tribulation for the believer (as elsewhere in Paul)
4. Shift in tone from 1 to 2 Thessalonians can be accounted for by the changing circumstances in the church	4. A much harsher tone is evident in 2 Thessalonians than in the first letter
5. Similarities in structure and wording with 1 Thessalonians, combined with important differences, make pseudonymity unlikely	5. Strong similarities in structure and wording make 2 Thessalonians redundant; why would Paul write such a similar letter?
6. Different eschatological emphases can be accounted for by different concerns in the church (in 1 Thessalonians, the problem is Christ's delay; in 2 Thessalonians, the issue is Christ's return may have already occurred)	6. Different eschatology than 1 Thessalonians (emphasis on signs rather than the imminence of the Second Coming)
7. Similarity in theological themes in 1 and 2 Thessalonians: eschatology, Christology, and theology proper	7. Higher Christology in 2 Thessalonians than elsewhere in Paul (2 Thess. 2:16; 3:5)
8. Emphasis on tradition and standards is apparent elsewhere in early Pauline writings (Rom. 6:17; 1 Cor. 11:23)	8. The concerns about false teaching and received tradition represent a later stage of the church
9. Identification of "man of lawlessness" with the Nero myth is pure speculation	9. Some identify the "man of lawlessness" with the myth of a resurrected Nero; this would date the letter after Paul
10. 2 Thessalonians is included in the Marcionite and Muratorian Canons	
11. Possible references in the Didache, Ignatius, and Polycarp; mentioned by Irenaeus by name	
Advocates	Advocates
Aus, Best, Bruce, Jewett, L. T. Johnson, Marshall, Morris	Bailey, Collins, Giblin, Holland, Hughes

Sources Consulted:

Achtemeier, Paul J., Joel B. Green, and Marianne Meye Thompson. *Introducing the New Testament: Its Literature and Theology*. Grand Rapids: Eerdmans, 2001.

Brown, Raymond E. *An Introduction to the New Testament*. New York: Doubleday, 1997.

Bruce, F. F. *1 and 2 Thessalonians*. Word Biblical Commentary. Vol. 45. Dallas: Word Books, 1982. [CD-ROM].

Guthrie, Donald. *New Testament Introduction*. 4th rev. ed. Downers Grove, Ill.: InterVarsity, 1990.

Thomas, Robert L. "1, 2 Thessalonians." In *The Expositor's Bible Commentary: With the New International Version of the Holy Bible*. Vol. 11. Edited by Frank Gaebelein. Grand Rapids: Zondervan, 1978.

Arguments concerning the Pauline Authorship of the Pastoral Epistles

Arguments For	Arguments Against
1. Pastoral Epistles appear in the Muratorian Canon; by the time of Irenaeus the Pastoral Epistles were considered Pauline	1. The Pastorals do not appear in the Marcionite Canon or the Chester Beatty Papyri (middle third century)
2. Paul's subject matter, age, and experience may account for the unique vocabulary in the Pastoral Epistles	2. Approximately one third of the words in the Pastorals do not appear elsewhere in Paul
3. Paul may have used a secretary for the actual writing of the letter	3. The overall style of writing is different than Paul's other letters
4. The heresy under discussion is not necessarily full-blown Gnosticism; the error just as well may have been a variant form of Judaism, which fits the first century context of Paul	4. Gnostic heresy under discussion (2 Tim. 2:17–18) represents later church concerns, not the problems of the middle first century
5. Acts 14:23; 20:17; 1 Thess. 5:17; and Phil. 1:1 show organizational concerns in Paul's writing and ministry	5. Paul's undisputed letters give little evidence of an advanced ecclesiology (e.g., the Corinthian church)
6. Ephesian church may have been ten years old by the time of 1 and 2 Timothy; the prohibition concerning new converts is not repeated in Titus, where a younger church is more likely	6. Prohibition of "new convert" from leadership (1 Tim. 3:6) reflects an established (i.e., older) stage of the church
7. Several points of contact between the Pastoral Epistles and Paul's farewell address to the Ephesian elders (Acts 20:17–38)	7. The theological issues now being raised (church order, ministerial qualifications, etc.) are different than those addressed in earlier writings
8. Paul's relationship with Timothy and Titus indicated in the Pastoral Epistles corresponds with that suggested in 1 Cor. 4:17; Phil. 2:19–23; and 2 Cor. 2:13; 7:6, 13	8. Key theological ideas such as the cross or Christ as the Son do not appear
9. Some scholars posit Paul's release from prison after Acts 28, a two-year journey with stops in Crete and Ephesus, the writing of 1 Timothy and Titus from Macedonia, and a second imprisonment, resulting in 2 Timothy	9. Pastoral Epistles do not fit within the chronology given in Acts; no clear evidence of a second Roman imprisonment in the New Testament
10. Clement of Rome and Eusebius refer to multiple imprisonments of Paul	
11. Paul is identified as the author of each letter (1 Tim. 1:1; 2 Tim. 1:1; Titus 1:4)	
Advocates	**Advocates**
Ellis, Guthrie, J. N. D. Kelly, Lock, Meinertz, Schlatter, Fee, Lightfoot	Holtzmann, Kümmel, P. N. Harrison, Goodspeed, Barrett, Conzelmann

Sources Consulted:

Brown, Raymond E. *An Introduction to the New Testament*. New York: Doubleday, 1997.

Earle, Ralph. "1, 2 Timothy." In *The Expositor's Bible Commentary: With the New International Version of the Holy Bible*. Vol. 11. Edited by Frank Gaebelein. Grand Rapids: Zondervan, 1978.

Guthrie, Donald. *New Testament Introduction*. 4th rev. ed. Downers Grove, Ill.: InterVarsity, 1990.

Lea, Thomas D. and Hayne P. Griffin. *1, 2 Timothy, Titus*. New American Commentary. Vol. 34. Nashville: Broadman and Holman, 1992.

Theories concerning the Authorship of Hebrews

Paul	
Advocates: Clement of Alexandria, Origen, Eusebius, Jerome, Augustine, Thomas Aquinas, Moses Stuart, W. Leonard	
## Arguments For	## Arguments Against
1. Circumstances in Hebrews 13 are similar to those of Paul in the accepted Pauline letters. Compare the following: Heb. 13:23 with Paul's friendship with Timothy. Heb. 13:18 with Rom. 15:30; 2 Cor. 1:11; Acts 23:1; 24:16; 2 Cor. 1:12; 1 Tim. 3:9; 2 Tim. 1:3. Heb. 13:19 with Philem. 22; Phil. 1:24–25. Heb. 13:20, 25 with Rom. 15:33; 1 Thess. 5:28; 2 Thess. 3:18.	1. Other individuals in the party of Paul could have had similar relationships to that expressed in the Pauline letters.
2. There are similar ideas in Hebrews to those in the Pauline letters: Christology: Heb. 1:3 with Col. 1:15. Heb. 1:2–3, 10–12 with Col. 1:16–17; 1 Cor. 8:6. Heb. 1:4–14; 2:14–17 with Phil. 2:5–11; Eph. 1:20–23; 3; Heb. 2:9; 9:26; 10:12 with 1 Tim. 2:6; Eph. 5:2; 1 Cor. 15:3. Two Covenants: Heb. 10:1 with Col. 2:16–17. Heb. 8:1–6; 4:1–2 with 1 Cor. 10:11. Heb. 7:18 with Rom. 8:3. Heb. 7:19; 8:8–13 with 2 Cor. 3:9–11.	2. The thoughts of the epistle are often dissimilar from the apostle's. The expressions "Jesus Christ," "Our Lord Jesus Christ," "Christ Jesus," and "the Lord" are absent, though these are used hundreds of times by Paul. The mention of the high priesthood in Hebrews is never mentioned by Paul. The mention of argument and manner of citing the OT is different from Paul's. Also, the writer of Hebrews uses only the LXX, while Paul uses also the Hebrew text. The author and Paul share basic apostolic teaching, nothing more.
3. Several terms in Hebrews are similar to those in the Pauline letters: Heb. 1:5 with Acts 13:33 (quotation is used by Paul and Hebrews to refer to Christ, but used nowhere else in NT). Heb. 2:4 with 1 Cor. 12:4, 6, 11. Heb. 2:10 with Rom. 11:36; Col. 1:16; 1 Cor. 8:6. Heb. 2:16 with Gal. 3:29; 4:16. Heb. 4:12 with Eph. 6:17. Heb. 6:3 with 1 Cor. 16:7. Heb. 10:19 with Rom. 5:2; Eph. 2:18; 3:12.	3. The style and language of Hebrews are quite different from those of the acknowledged works of Paul. About 168 words in Hebrews occur nowhere else in the NT and an additional 124 do not appear in Paul's works. Also, Hebrews is in polished, precise Greek in contrast to the uneven style of the apostle.
4. Pauline authorship was accepted by Clement of Alexandria near the end of the second century, and Hebrews was found in a collection of Paul's books in Egypt (P[46]). Eusebius thought Hebrews was written by Paul in Hebrew and translated into Greek by Luke. This was later argued also by Aquinas. Pauline authorship was the dominant view from the fifth century to the Reformation, especially due to the influence of Jerome and Augustine.	4. The historical evidence for Pauline authorship is meager. The Muratorian Canon, Irenaeus, Hippolytus, and Gaius of Rome did not regard the letter as Pauline. Eusebius (c. A.D. 325) says that several Romans did not consider the work Pauline. Ambrosiaster (late 4th century) considered the letter an anonymous work. Hesitancy to give full Pauline status is indicated by the separate mention of Hebrews from the thirteen epistles of Paul at the Synod of Hippo in 393 and the Third Synod of Carthage in 397. The epistle gives no indication of being a translation.

Arguments For	Arguments Against
5. Peter may have been referring to Hebrews in his statements about Paul in 2 Peter 3:15, a reference to Peter's audience of Jewish Christians.	5. Peter's audience more likely was a general audience and a scattered one, whereas Hebrews was written to Jews at a specific locality.
	6. The lack of appeal to apostolic authority is unusual if the book is Paul's; cf. Rom. 1:1; 1 Cor. 1:1, et al.
	7. Hebrews 2:3 seems to convey the thoughts of a second- or third-generation Christian who is dependent on another's authority, in contrast to the independent authority of Paul; cf. Gal. 1:12.
	8. Paul does not add a personal signature as was his custom (cf. 2 Thess. 3:17).

Luke

Advocates: Origen mentions that some in his day held to Lucan authorship; Calvin (?); F. Delitzsch

Arguments For	Arguments Against
1. There are similarities in style between Luke's writings and Hebrews.	1. The similarity of style may be accounted for by a "community of atmosphere." Moreover, Hebrews is a more polished work than Luke–Acts.
2. The Pauline thoughts in Hebrews could be explained readily, since Luke was a close companion of the apostle.	2. Luke was only one among many in close association with the apostle; so, though it makes him a possible candidate for authorship, he is only one among many.
3. The recorded speech of Stephen by Luke closely resembles the book of Hebrews: reviews of Jewish history, the call of Abraham, nonpossession of the land, the tabernacle divinely ordained, the law mediated through angels, the call to "go out," the idea of the "living Word," allusion to Joshua, and the heavenward call.	3. The similarities between Hebrews and Stephen's speech argue more for Stephen as author than Luke, unless it is presumed that Luke wrote the speech.

Apollos	
Advocates: Martin Luther, T. Zahn, C. Spicq, T. W. Manson, W. F. Howard, A. T. Robertson	
Arguments For	**Arguments Against**
1. Apollos was an Alexandrian Jew. The author of Hebrews was a Jew, probably with Alexandrian influence.	1. Though the characteristics and circumstances demonstrate that Apollos could have written the epistle, since there are no extant writings of Apollos for comparison, there is no evidence that he did in fact write it. Another in the first century, anonymous to us, with the same kind of qualifications may have written it.
2. Apollos was a learned man. The author of Hebrews was a learned man, being the NT writer with the best Greek composition in style and logic.	2. No ancient tradition supports Apollos as author. In fact, wasn't Luther the first to propose him? The failure of the Alexandrian church to preserve a tradition is hard to understand if Apollos wrote it.
3. Apollos accurately taught about Jesus (Acts 18:25). The writer of Hebrews gives a precise and accurate presentation of Jesus.	3. Acts 18:24ff. says nothing about Apollos being trained in Philonic thought, that which Hebrews appears to reflect.
4. Apollos is portrayed as one who powerfully used the Old Testament (Acts 18:24). The author of Hebrews argues strongly from the OT, displaying a masterful understanding.	
5. Apollos was fervent in spirit. This is similar to the writer of the epistle, who writes with passion and "boldness."	
6. Apollos had an excellent reputation in the early church (cf. Acts 18; 1 Cor. 1:12). The contact of Paul and Apollos might explain Pauline expressions and thoughts and also account for the mention of Timothy in 13:23.	

Barnabas	
Advocates: Tertullian (seemingly expressing common consent), Gregory of Elvira, B. Weiss, G. Salmon, F. Blass, C. R. Gregory, K. Bornhäusen	
Arguments For	**Arguments Against**
1. As a Levite from Cyprus (Acts 4:36) Barnabas was qualified to write on the Levitical regulations of the law.	1. The Alexandrian character of the book makes it unlikely to have come from a Cyprian Jew.
2. There may be a connection between Barnabas as a "son of exhortation" (Acts 4:36) and the "word of exhortation" (Heb. 13:22) given by the author of Hebrews.	2. Historical attestation is meager and all Western. One would expect more, since Barnabas was a well-known figure.
3. The authorship of Barnabas is attested by Tertullian, who seems to express a common (possibly a Roman) agreement, and by Gregory of Elvira and Philastrius (fourth-century bishop of Brescia).	3. It is unlikely that an early disciple in Jerusalem would have written Hebrews 2:3.
	4. Barnabas produced no works with which to compare Hebrews, so the internal evidence is mute.

Priscilla and Aquila (Priscilla dominant)	
Advocates: A. Harnack, some modern feminists	
Arguments For	**Arguments Against**
1. Their quality as teachers was attested by teaching Apollos (Acts 18:26).	1. Their success as teachers would qualify them as possible authors, but they left no writings to compare with Hebrews.
2. These two were closely associated with Timothy (Acts 18:5; 19:22; 1 Cor. 16:10, 19).	2. They are only two among many associated with Paul and Timothy.
3. If salutations in Rom. 16:3–16 are intended for Rome and if Hebrews was written to Rome, it is significant that they hosted a house-church in Rome (Rom. 16:5; cf. 1 Cor. 16:10, 19).	3. Being from the church at Rome in no way makes them likely authors. The salutation is ambiguous; and if it is a greeting to those in Rome, many others would also qualify as possible authors.
4. The transitions between "we" and "I" might be explained by dual authorship.	4. The use of the plural is not solid proof for plural authorship, since Hebrews 13:19 is emphatically in the singular as is 11:32 and 13:22–23.

Arguments For	Arguments Against
5. The antifeminist tendency in much of postapostolic church, for example the Western text (especially Codex D), might account for the disappearance of the author's name.	5. The significant position of women in the ministries of Jesus, Paul, and the subapostolic church reveals a proper attitude of the church to women, even though some leaders may have been negative.
6. The mention of women in the list of heroes in Hebrews 11 may reflect a woman's interest.	6. The mention of women in the list of heroes could also have been written by a man; cf. Luke's books.
7. The pilgrim theme in 11:13–16 may speak to their being outcasts from Rome under Claudius.	7. There is no historical evidence to back the claim.
8. The interest in the tabernacle may come from the fact that they were tentmakers.	8. The interest in the tabernacle is typological and not from a tentmaker's perspective.
	9. The participle in Hebrews 11:32, which in this case indicates the sex of the author, reveals the author to be masculine.
	10. The authoritative tone of the epistle would speak against Priscilla as author in view of New Testament teaching, especially that of Paul (1 Cor. 14:34–35; 1 Tim. 2:11ff).
Clement of Rome	
Advocates: Erasmus, K. and S. Lake (?), Calvin (?)	
There are striking similarities between Clement's letter to the Corinthians (I Clement) and the Book of Hebrews; cf. I Clement 26.	1. The parallel between I Clement and Hebrews may be explained simply as evidence of Clement's familiarity with Hebrews.
	2. The style and ability of the two writers are considerably different, with the writer of Hebrews being far superior.
	3. The probable great difference of time between Hebrews and I Clement (30 years most likely) makes Clement an unlikely author of the epistle.

Perhaps Origen got it right when he said, "But who wrote the epistle, in truth, God knows" (quoted by Eusebius in *Church History* 6.25.14).

Arguments concerning the Petrine Authorship of 2 Peter

Arguments For	Arguments Against
1. Other pseudonymous works claiming Petrine authorship (The Apocalypse of Peter, The Gospel of Peter, and The Acts of Peter) were not considered canonical	1. If Peter was the author, the church would have accepted the letter sooner
2. May be reflected in Clement of Rome and the Epistle of Barnabas	2. Eusebius doubted the authenticity of 2 Peter; no definite mention of 2 Peter until Origen
3. 1 and 2 Peter are omitted in the Muratorian Canon, but 1 Peter is regarded by most as authentic	3. 2 Peter does not appear in the Muratorian Canon
4. 2 Peter claims to have been written by Simon Peter (1:1; 1:14; 1:16–18)	4. Unlike 1 Peter, 2 Peter contains almost no Old Testament allusions
5. "Simeon" (1:1) represents a Hebraic form of Simon, and one that does not appear in 1 Peter; this is not a likely form to be used by a pseudipigrapher	5. Over 60% of the vocabulary in 2 Peter is not found in 1 Peter
6. Author mentions a previous epistle (3:1) and intimacy with the apostle Paul (3:15)	6. Literary dependence on Jude, a document dated by some scholars after Peter's death
7. Reference to "all his [Paul's] letters" may mean only those letters known at the time of writing	7. Reference to "all his [Paul's] letters" suggests a later period of development and the establishment of a set body of Paul's work
8. Hellenistic language is not overly developed; rudimentary knowledge of the terms is not unreasonable for even a Galilean fisherman	8. Language is Hellenistic, unlikely for a Galilean fisherman
9. Different literary style between 1 and 2 Peter may be accounted for the by the use of one or more scribes	9. Significant differences in literary style between 1 and 2 Peter
10. The delay of the Second Coming was both a first and second-century problem	10. The delay of the Second Coming represents a later period
11. Different thematic emphases may be accounted for by differing purposes	11. Thematic differences between 1 Peter (the cross, resurrection, ascension, and baptism) and 2 Peter (Second Coming)
12. The "Gnosticism" under discussion is not clearly described and may represent only an incipient form	12. Some think second-century Gnosticism is under discussion in 2 Peter
Advocates	**Advocates**
Guthrie, Blum	Baukham, Brown, Kelly, and most contemporary scholars

Sources Consulted:

Baukham, Richard J. *Jude, 2 Peter*. Word Biblical Commentary. Vol. 42. Dallas: Word Books, 1983. [CD-ROM].

Blum, Edwin A. "1, 2 Peter." In *The Expositor's Bible Commentary: With the New International Version of the Holy Bible*. Vol. 12. Edited by Frank Gaebelein. Grand Rapids: Zondervan, 1982.

Brown, Raymond E. *An Introduction to the New Testament*. New York: Doubleday, 1997.

Guthrie, Donald. *New Testament Introduction*. 4th rev. ed. Downers Grove, Ill.: InterVarsity, 1990.

Arguments concerning the Relationship between 2 Peter and Jude

	2 Peter	Jude
Parallel Passages	2:1–18	4–13
	3:1–3	16–18

Arguments for the Priority of 2 Peter	Arguments for the Priority of Jude
1. Jude 4 and 17 are considered references to 2 Peter	1. If 2 Peter already existed, the publication of an extract of 2 Peter with only a different salutation and doxology makes little sense
2. Peter refers to the false teachers in present and future tense; Jude uses only present tense; what Peter was experiencing and foresaw in the future, Jude was presently combating	2. If 2 Peter already existed, the republication of this material under the name of Jude, an obscure figure in comparison to Peter, seems unlikely
3. Inexplicable why an apostle would take over the writings of a lesser known person	3. The lack of introductory material gives evidence of spontaneity and priority
4. 2 Peter appears to be a very unified document	4. Inclusion of apocryphal books (and their absence in 2 Peter) suggests the author of 2 Peter has excised these unorthodox references
	5. The midrashic structure of Jude would not have been employed if using another source
	6. The midrash of Jude is carefully composed (in contrast to 2 Peter's rather simple and loose form)
Advocates	**Advocates**
Luther, Spitta, Zahn, Bigg, Falconcer	Most modern commentators

Sources Consulted:

Baukham, Richard J. *Jude, 2 Peter*. Word Biblical Commentary. Vol. 42. Dallas: Word Books, 1983. [CD-ROM].

Brown, Raymond E. *An Introduction to the New Testament*. New York: Doubleday, 1997.

Guthrie, Donald. *New Testament Introduction*. 4th rev. ed. Downers Grove, Ill.: InterVarsity, 1990.

Interpretations of Revelation

	1–3	4–19	20–22
Preterist	Historic churches	Symbolic of contemporary (1st century) conditions	Symbolic of heaven and victory
Idealist	Historic churches	Symbolic of conflict of good and evil	Victory of good
Historicist	Historic churches	Symbolic of events of history: fall of Rome, Mohammedanism, papacy, Reformation	Final judgment, millennium (?), eternal state
Futurist	Historic churches and/or seven stages of church history	Future tribulation; concentrated judgments on world and on Antichrist; coming of Christ	Millennial kingdom; judgment of wicked dead; eternal state

Theological Perspectives on Revelation

	1–3	4–19	20–22
Postmillennial or Preterist	Historic churches	Generally historicist	Victory of Christianity over the world
Amillennial or Idealist	Historic churches	Generally historicist	Coming of Christ; judgment; eternal state
Premillennial	Historic churches representative of the whole spectrum of churches in every age	Generally futurist	Literal millennial reign; judgment of great white throne; New Jerusalem
Apocalyptic	Historic churches	Generally preterist	Symbolic of heaven and victory

Theories of Literary Structures of Revelation

Literary Construction: 6:1–17; 8:1–9:21 and 11:15–19; 15:1–16:12 and 16:17–21:27

	Seals			Trumpets			Bowls		
	1-6	( )	7	1-6	( )	7	1-6	( )	7
A parenthesis between 6th and 7th judgments in each series:		7:1–17			10:1–11:14			16:13–16	
A parenthesis between the trumpet judgment and the bowl series:						12:1–14:20			
A parenthesis between the bowl series and the description of the second coming of Jesus:									17:1–19:10

Suggested Interrelationships of the Seals, Trumpets, and Bowls:

Judgements are seen as occurring simultaneously, with repetition showing the intensification of the judgments.

Seals
Trumpets
Bowls

This consecutive arrangement envisions a total of twenty-one judgments.

Seals • Trumpets • Bowls

This telescopic arrangement has the seventh seal introducing the trumpet series and being explained by it, and the seventh trumpet introduces the bowl series and is explained by it. So, the seven bowls equal the seventh trumpet and the seven trumpets are the seventh seal.

7th Seal

1 2 3 4 5 6
Seals

7th Trumpet

1 2 3 4 5 6
Trumpets

1 2 3 4 5 6 7
Bowls

Adapted from Robert G. Gromacki, *New Testament Survey* (Grand Rapids: Baker, 1974), by permission.

Arguments concerning the Date of Revelation

Arguments for a Neronian Date (A.D. 64–70)	Arguments for a Domitianic Date (c. A.D. 95)
1. References to persecution in Revelation could accord with the known persecutions under Nero	1. Nero's persecution was apparently limited to Rome; although widespread persecution did not occur under Domitian, investigations away from Rome were more common
2. References to the Temple (Rev. 11), if taken literally, may indicate a date before A.D. 70	2. Degenerate state of the churches in Rev. 2–3 reflects later rather than earlier date
3. No reference in Revelation to the siege and destruction of Jerusalem	3. Use of "Babylon" for Rome occurs only after A.D. 70 (like Babylon in 587 B.C., Rome captured Jerusalem and destroyed the Temple)
4. Nero accepted divine attributions during his lifetime	4. Domitian accepted divine attributions during his lifetime; Domitian demanded he be addressed as "our Lord and God"
5. 666 can be calculated on the basis of the Hebrew transcription of the name Neron Caesar	5. The reference to seven kings (Rev. 17:9-11) most likely refers to a time after Nero
6. The Muratorian Canon and Monarchian Prologues indicate early dates (though pre-Pauline)	6. The myth that Nero did not really die or was resurrected may be reflected in Rev. 13:3, 12, 14; such a myth would take time to achieve widespread belief
	7. Irenaeus clearly asserted that Revelation was written during the close of Domitian's reign
	8. Eusebius reports persecution and martyrdoms during the reign of Domitian
	9. *I Clement* suggests a persecution in his own day paralleling the days of Nero
	10. Pliny the Younger in A.D. 110 spoke of Christians who claimed to have abandoned the faith twenty years earlier (c. A.D. 90)
Advocates	**Advocates**
Eckhardt, Stolt, Bell, Wilson, Rowland	Collins, Müller, Roloff, Koester, Hemer

Sources Consulted:

Achtemeier, Paul J., Joel B. Green, and Marianne Meye Thompson. *Introducing the New Testament: Its Literature and Theology.* Grand Rapids: Eerdmans, 2001.

Aune, David E. *Revelation 1–5.* Word Biblical Commentary. Vol. 52. Dallas: Word Books, 1997. [CD-ROM].

Brown, Raymond E. *An Introduction to the New Testament.* New York: Doubleday, 1997.

Guthrie, Donald. *New Testament Introduction.* 4th rev. ed. Downers Grove, Ill.: InterVarsity, 1990.

Johnson, Alan F. "Revelation." In *The Expositor's Bible Commentary: With the New International Version of the Holy Bible.* Vol. 12. Edited by Frank Gaebelein. Grand Rapids: Zondervan, 1982.

Content and Correlation of the Judgments of Seals, Trumpets, and Bowls

Number	Seals Opened by the Lamb	Trumpets Blown by seven angels	Bowls Poured by seven angels
1.	White horse: conqueror	Hail and fire; 1/3 of vegetation burnt	Sores
2.	Red horse: war	Mountain of fire; 1/3 of creatures in sea destroyed	Sea becomes blood; all marine life dies
3.	Black horse: famine	Star called wormwood falls; 1/3 of fresh water poisoned	Fresh water turned to blood
4.	Pale horse: death	Partial darkness; 1/3 of sun, moon, and stars	Scorching sun burns men
		HIATUS: Last three trumpets announced as woes	
5.	Martyrs reassured	Woe #1: Angel releases locusts from abyss	Darkness on beast's kingdom
6.	Great day of wrath: earthquake, signs in heaven	Woe #2: Four angels loosed at Euphrates; they slay 1/3 of earth's population	Euphrates dries up; kings assemble for war at Armageddon
	HIATUS: Sealing of 144,000	HIATUS: Mystery of God to be concluded with seventh trumpet	
7.	1/2 hour of silence: introduction of trumpets	Announcement of the Lord's victory	Severe earthquake and great hail

Adapted from Robert G. Gromacki, *New Testament Survey* (Grand Rapids: Baker, 1974), by permission.

Bibliography

Achtemeier, Paul J., Joel B. Green, and Marianne Meye Thompson. *Introducing the New Testament: Its Literature and Theology*. Grand Rapids: Eerdmans, 2001.

Adams, Jay E. *Audience Adaptations in the Sermons and Speeches of Paul*. Grand Rapids: Baker, 1976.

Aland, Kurt, ed. *Synopsis of the Four Gospels*. New York: United Bible Societies, 1985.

Arndt, William F., F. Wilbur Gingrich, and F. W. Danker. *A Greek-English. Lexicon of the New Testament and Other Early Christian Literature*. 3rd edition. Chicago: University of Chicago Press, 2000.

Arnold, William Thomas. *The Roman System of Provincial Administration to the Accession of Constantine the Great*. 3rd edition. Revised by E. S. Bouchier. Freeport, NY: Books for Libraries, 1971.

Aune, David E. *Revelation 1–5*. Word Biblical Commentary. Vol. 52. Dallas: Word Books, 1997. [CD-ROM].

Barclay, William. *The First Three Gospels*. Philadelphia: Westminster, 1966.

Barker, William Pierson. *Personalities Around Jesus*. Westwood, N.J.: Revell, 1963.

Barnes, Rev. C. R. *Handbook of Bible Bibliography*. New York: Hunt and Eaton, 1980.

Baukham, Richard J. *Jude, 2 Peter*. Word Biblical Commentary. Vol. 42. Dallas: Word Books, 1983. [CD-ROM].

Blomberg, Craig. *The Historical Reliability of the Gospels*. Downers Grove, Ill.: InterVarsity, 1987.

Blum, Edwin A. "1, 2 Peter." In *The Expositor's Bible Commentary*. Vol. 12. Edited by Frank E. Gaebelein. Grand Rapids: Zondervan, 1982.

———. "Jude." In *The Expositor's Bible Commentary*. Vol. 12. Edited by Frank E. Gaebelein. Grand Rapids: Zondervan, 1982.

Boak, Arthur E. R. *A History of Rome to 565 A.D.* New York: Macmillan, 1943.

Bock, Darrell L. "The Words of Jesus in the Gospels: Live, Jive, or Memorex?" In *Jesus Under Fire*. Edited by Michael J. Wilkins and J. P. Moreland, 73–100. Grand Rapids: Zondervan, 1995.

Bouquet, Alan Coates. *Everyday Life in New Testament Times*. New York: Scribner, 1954.

Brandon, S. G. F. "The Date of the Markan Gospel." *New Testament Studies* 7 (1961): 126–41.

Bratcher, Robert G., ed. *Old Testament Quotations in the New Testament*. London: United Bible Societies, 1967.

Bratcher, Robert G., and John A. Thompson. *Bible Index*. London: United Bible Societies, 1970.

Brownrigg, Ronald. *Who's Who in the New Testament*. New York: Holt, Rinehart and Winston, 1971.

Bruce, A. B. *The Parabolic Teachings of Christ*. London: Hodder and Stoughton, 1904.

Bruce, F. F. *Israel and the Nations, from the Exodus to the Fall of the Second Temple*. Grand Rapids: Eerdmans, 1963.

———. *Jesus and Christian Origins outside the New Testament*. Grand Rapids: Eerdmans, 1974.

———. *New Testament History*. Sunbury on Thames: Nelson, 1969.

Buttrick, George Arthur, ed. *The Interpreter's Dictionary of the Bible: An Illustrated Encyclopedia*. New York: Abingdon, 1962.

Carson, D. A., and Douglas J. Moo. *An Introduction to the New Testament*. 2nd edition. Grand Rapids: Zondervan, 2006.

Cary, M., and H. H. Scullard. *A History of Rome Down to the Reign of Constantine*. New York: St. Martins', 1975.

Cary, Max. *A History of the Greek World from 323 to 146 B.C.* London: Methuen, 1932.

Charles, Robert Henry. *The Apocrypha and Pseudepigrapha of the Old Testament in English*. Oxford: Clarendon, 1913.

Charlesworth, James H., ed. *The Old Testament Pseudepigrapha*. 2 Vols. Garden City, N.Y.: Doubleday, 1983.

———. *The Pseudepigrapha and Modern Research*. Missoula, Mont.: Scholars, 1976.

Cheney, Johnston M., and Stanley Ellisen, eds. *The Life of Christ in Stereo*. Portland, OR: Western Conservative Baptist Seminary, 1969.

Conybeare, William John and J. S. Howson. *The Life and Epistles of St. Paul*. Grand Rapids: Eerdmans, 1989.

Coogan, Michael D. and Bruce M. Metzger, eds. *The Oxford Companion to the Bible*. New York: Oxford University Press, 1993.

Cook, R. M. *The Greeks until Alexander*. New York: Praeger, 1962.

Cook, S. A., F. E. Adcock, and M. P. Charlesworth, eds. *The Cambridge Ancient History*. Vols. 6–11. Cambridge, England: Cambridge University Press, 1923–39.

Crapps, Robert W., Edgar V. McKnight, and David A. Smith. *Introduction to the New Testament*. New York: Wiley, 1969.

Cribbs, F. Lamar. "A Reassessment of the Date of Origin and the Destination of the Gospel of John." *Journal of Biblical Literature* 89 (March 1970): 38–55.

Davies, W. D. *Invitation to the New Testament*. Garden City, N.Y.: Doubleday, 1969.

Dodd, C. H. Apostolic Preaching and Its Developments. London: Hodder and Stoughton, 1944. Reprint, Grand Rapids: Baker, 1980.

_____. *The Parables of the Kingdom*. New York: Scribner, 1961.

Douglas, J. D., ed. *The New Bible Dictionary*. 3rd edition. Revised by D. R. W. Wood. Downers Grove, Ill.: InterVarsity, 1996.

Drane, John W. *Jesus and the Four Gospels*. San Francisco: Harper and Row, 1979.

Earle, Ralph. "1, 2 Timothy." In *The Expositor's Bible Commentary*. Vol. 11. Edited by Frank E. Gaebelein. Grand Rapids: Zondervan, 1978.

Ellis, E. Earle. *Paul's Use of the Old Testament*. Grand Rapids: Eerdmans, 1957.

Ellisen, Stanley. *Bible Workbook Part VI: The Synoptic Gospels*. Portland, Ore.: Western Conservative Baptist Seminary, 1969.

_____. *Biography of a Great Planet*. Wheaton, IL: Tyndale, 1975.

_____. *The Book of Romans: God's Philosophy of Salvation, Progressive Bible Studies, Step 1*. Portland, Ore.: Western Conservative Baptist Seminary, 1971.

_____. "Studies in Specialized Areas of Exposition (Types and Parables)." Class notes for BL 337, Western Conservative Baptist Seminary, 1979.

Finegan, Jack. *The Archaeology of the New Testament: The Life of Jesus and the Beginning of the Early Church*. Princeton: Princeton University Press, 1992.

_____. *Handbook of Biblical Chronology: Principles of Time Reckoning in the Ancient World and Problems of Chronology in the Bible*. Peabody, Mass.: Hendrickson, 1998.

Foster, Lewis A. "The Chronology of the New Testament." In Frank E. Gaebelein, ed. *Expositor's Bible Commentary*. Vol. 1. Grand Rapids: Zondervan, 1979.

_____. "The Metrology of the New Testament." In Frank E. Gabelein, ed. *Expositor's Bible Commentary*. Vol. 1. Grand Rapids: Zondervan, 1979.

France, R. T. *Jesus and the Old Testament*. London: Tyndale, 1971.

Freeman-Greenville, Stewart Parker. *Chronology of World History: A Calendar of Principal Events from 3000 B.C. to A.D. 1973*. London: Collins, 1975.

Funk, Robert W., Roy W. Hoover, and the Jesus Seminar. *The Five Gospels: The Search for the Authentic Words of Jesus*. New York: Polebridge Press, 1993.

Goodspeed, Edgar J. *An Introduction to the New Testament*. Chicago: University of Chicago Press, 1950.

Grant, Frederick C. *Harper's Annotated Bible*. New York: Harper, 1955.

The Greek New Testament, 4th revised edition. Edited by Barbara Aland, Kurt Aland, Johannes Karavidopoulos, Carlo M. Martini, and Bruce M. Metzger, in cooperation with the Institute for New Testament Textual Research, Münster/Westphalia. Stuttgart: Deutsche Bibelgesellschaft, 1993.

Greenlee, J. Harold. *Introduction to New Testament Textual Criticism*. Grand Rapids: Eerdmans, 1964.

Gromacki, Robert Glenn. *New Testament Survey*. Grand Rapids: Baker, 1989.

Grun, Bernard. *The Timetables of History: A Horizontal Linkage of People and Events, Based on Werner Stein's Kulturfahrplan*. New York: Simon and Schuster, 1975.

Gundry, Robert Horton. *A Survey of the New Testament*. 4th edition. Grand Rapids: Zondervan, 2003.

Guthrie, Donald. *New Testament Introduction*. 4th rev. ed. Downers Grove, Ill.: InterVarsity, 1990.

Harrison, Everett Falconer. *Introduction to the New Testament*. Revised edition. Grand Rapids: Eerdmans, 1971.

Heard, Richard. *An Introduction to the New Testament*. New York: Harper, 1950.

Hiebert, David Edmond. *An Introduction to the Non-Pauline Epistles*. Chicago: Moody Press, 1962.

_____. *Personalities around Paul*. Chicago: Moody Press, 1973.

Hobbs, H. H. "The Miraculous Element in Matthew." *Southwestern Journal of Theology* 5 (1962): 41–54.

Hoehner, Harold W. *Chronological Aspects of the Life of Christ*. Grand Rapids: Zondervan, 1977.

_____. "A Chronological Table of the Apostolic Age." A handout by the author, April 1972.

_____. *Herod Antipas*. Grand Rapids: Zondervan, 1980.

Honoré, A. M. "A Statistical Study of the Synoptic Problem." In *The Synoptic Problem and Q: Selected Studies from Novum Testamentum*. Edited by David E. Orton. Boston: Brill, 1999. 70–122.

Hornblower, Simon, and Antony Spawforth, eds. *The Oxford Classical Dictionary*. 3rd edition. Revised. New York: Oxford University Press, 2003.

Jaubert, Annie. *The Date of the Last Supper*. Translated by Isaac Rafferty. New York: Alba, 1965.

Jensen, Irving L. *1 Corinthians*. Chicago: Moody, 1972.

_____. *John*. Chicago: Moody, 1970.

_____. *The Life of Christ*. Moody Bible Institute Correspondence School, December 2–4. Chicago: Moody Bible Institute, 1975.

Jeremias, Joachim. *Jerusalem in the Time of Jesus*. Translated by F. H. Cave and C. H. Cave. Philadelphia: Fortress, 1969.

_____. *The Parables of Jesus*. Translated by. New York: Scribner, 1963.

Johnson, Alan. "Assurance for Man: The Fallacy of Translating *Anaidea* by 'Persistence' in Luke 11:5–8." *Journal of the Evangelical Theological Society* 22, no. 2 (June 1979): 123–31.

_____. "Revelation." In *The Expositor's Bible Commentary*. Vol. 12. Edited by Frank E. Gaebelein. Grand Rapids: Zondervan, 1982.

Jones, A. H. M., ed. *A History of Rome Through the Fifth Century, Volume II: The Empire*. New York: Walker, 1970.

Kee, Howard D., Franklin W. Young, and Karlfried Froehlich. *Understanding the New Testament*. Englewood Cliffs, N.J.: Prentice-Hall, 1957.

Kümmel, Werner Georg. *An Introduction to the New Testament*. Translated by Howard Clark Kee. Nashville: Abingdon, 1975.

Lake, Kirsopp. *An Introduction to the New Testament*. London: Christophers, 1948.

Laney, J. Carl. "Selective Geographical Problems in the Life of Christ." Th.D. diss., Dallas Theological Seminary, 1977.

LaSor, William Sanford. *The Dead Sea Scrolls and the Christian Faith*. Chicago: Moody, 1956.

Lea, Thomas D., and Hayne P. Griffin. *1, 2 Timothy, Titus*. New American Commentary. Vol. 34. Nashville: Broadman and Holman, 1992.

Lightfoot, J. B. *Saint Paul's Epistle to the Galatians*. London: Macmillian, 1865.

Lincoln, Andrew T. *Ephesians*. Word Biblical Commentary. Vol. 42. Dallas: Word Books, 1990. [CD-ROM].

Lohse, Eduard. *The New Testament Environment*. Translated by John E. Steely. Nashville: Abingdon, 1976.

Longenecker, Richard N. "Acts." In *The Expositor's Bible Commentary*. Vol. 9. Edited by Frank E. Gaebelein. Grand Rapids: Zondervan, 1984.

_____. *Biblical Exegesis in the Apostolic Period*. 2nd edition. Grand Rapids: Eerdmans, 1999. [CD-ROM].

Machen, John Gresham. *The New Testament: An Introduction to Its Literature and History*. Edinburgh: Banner of Truth Trust, 1976.

Mansoor, Menahem. *The Dead Sea Scrolls*. Grand Rapids: Eerdmans, 1964.

Martin, Ralph. *The Acts, The Epistles, The Apocalypse*. New Testament Foundations: A Guide for Christian Students. Vol. 2. Grand Rapids: Eerdmans, 1978.

_____. *The Four Gospels*. New Testament Foundations: A Guide for Christian Students. Vol. 1. Grand Rapids: Eerdmans, 1975.

McCullough, William Stewart. *The History and Literature of the Palestinian Jews from Cyrus to Herod*. Toronto: University of Toronto Press, 1975.

Metzger, Bruce M. *The New Testament, Its Background, Growth and Content*. New York: Abingdon, 1965.

_____. *The Text of the New Testament: Its Transmission, Corruption, and Restoration*. 3rd edition. New York: Oxford University Press, 1992.

Miller, Merland Ray. "Timetables and Charts for the New Testament." Th.M. thesis. Portland, Ore.: Western Conservative Baptist Seminary, 1980.

Milsson, Martin P. *Greek Piety*. New York: Norton, 1969.

The Mishnah: Translated from the Hebrew with Introduction and Brief Explanatory Notes. Translated by Herbert Danby. London: Oxford University Press, 1974.

Moore, Ralph W. *The Roman Commonwealth*. Port Washington, N.Y.: Kennikat, 1969.

Morris, Leon. *Apocalyptic*. Grand Rapids: Eerdmans, 1972.

_____. *John*. New International Commentary of the New Testament. Grand Rapids: Eerdmans, 1971.

Moulton, W. F., and A. S. Geden, eds. *Concordance to the Greek Testament: According to the Texts of Westcott and Hort, Tischendorf, and the English Revisers*. 5th edition. Revised by H. K. Moulton. Edinburgh: T. and T. Clark, 1978.

Nicole, Roger. "The Old Testament in the New Testament." In *The Expositor's Bible Commentary*. Vol. 1. Edited by Frank E. Gaebelein. Grand Rapids: Zondervan, 1979.

Nix, William E., and Norman L. Geisler. *Introduction to the Bible*. Chicago: Moody, 1968.

O'Brien, Peter T. *Colossians, Philemon*. Word Biblical Commentary. Vol. 44. Dallas: Word Books, 1982. [CD-ROM].

Oesterley, W. O. E., and G. H. Box. *A Short Survey of the Literature of Rabbinical and Mediaeval Judaism*. New York: Macmillan, 1920.

Pellison, Maurice. *Roman Life in Pliny's Time*. New York: Chautauzana Century, 1897.

Pfeiffer, Charles F. *Between the Testaments*. Grand Rapids: Baker, 1959.

_____. *The Dead Sea Scrolls and the Bible*. Grand Rapids: Baker, 1969.

_____. *The Wycliffe Bible Encyclopedia*. Chicago: Moody, 1975.

_____. *The Wycliffe Historical Geography of Bible Lands*. Chicago: Moody, 1975.

Pfeiffer, R. H. *History of New Testament Times and an Introduction to the Apocrypha*. New York: Harper, 1949.

Pomeroy, Sarah B. *Goddesses, Whores, Wives, and Slaves*. New York: Schocken, 1975.

Rahlfs, Alfred, ed. *Septuagint*, 5th edition. Stuttgart: Deutsche Bibelgesellschaft, 1952.

Ramsay, William Mitchell. *The Cities of St. Paul: Their Influence on His Life and Thought*. London: Hodder and Stoughton, 1907. Reprint, Grand Rapids: Baker, 1949.

_____. *A Historical Commentary on St. Paul's Epistle to the Galatians*. London: Hodder and Stoughton, 1899. Reprint, Grand Rapids: Baker, 1965.

_____. *St. Paul the Traveller and the Roman Citizen*. London: Hodder and Stoughton, 1896.

Rendall, Frederic. "The Epistle to the Galatians." *The Expositor's Greek Testament*. Vol. 3. Edited by W. Robertson Nicoll. Grand Rapids: Eerdmans, 1967.

Robertson, A. T. *Chronological New Testament*. New York: Revell, 1904.

_____. *A Harmony of the Gospels*. New York: Harper, 1922.

Robinson, Cyril E. *A History of Rome*. New York: Crowell, n.d.

Rowley, H. H., and Matthew Black, eds. *Peake's Commentary on the Bible*. Revised by C. S. C. Williams. London: Nelson, 1962.

Russel, David Syme. *Between the Testaments*. Philadelphia: Westminster, 1976.

Ryrie Study Bible: New American Standard Bible. Expanded edition. Chicago: Moody Press, 1995.

Safrai, S. *The Jewish People in the First Century*. 2 vols. Assen: Van Gorcum, 1974–76.

Salmon, Edward T. *A History of the Roman World from 30 B.C. to A.D. 138*. London: Methuen, 1968.

Schiffman, Lawrence H. *From Text to Tradition: A History of Second Temple Judaism*. Hoboken, N.J.: Ktav Publishing, 1991.

Schubert, Paul. "The Final Cycle of Speeches in the Book of Acts." *Journal of Biblical Literature* 87 (1968): 1–16.

Schürer, Emil. *A History of the Jewish People in the Age of Jesus Christ* (175 B.C.–A.D. 135). 3 vols. Revised and edited by Fergus Millar and Geza Vermes. Edinburgh: Clark, 1973–87.

Sloan, William Wilson. *A Survey between the Testaments*. Paterson, N.J.: Littlefield, Adams, 1964.

Smith, Norman Henry. *The Jews from Cyrus to Herod*. New York, Abingdon, 1956.

Soulen, Richard N. *Handbook of Biblical Criticism*. Atlanta: John Knox, 1976.

Strack, Herman L., and G. Stemberger. *Introduction to the Talmud and Midrash*. Translated by Markus Bockmuehl. Minneapolis: Fortress, 1992.

Streeter, B. H. *The Four Gospels*. New York: Harper, 1933.

Sturz, Harry A. *The Byzantine Text-Type and New Testament Textural Criticism*. La Mirada, Calif.: Biola College Bookstore, 1972.

Swete, Henry Barclay. *An Introduction to the Old Testament in Greek*. New York: KTAV, 1968.

Tenney, Merrill C. *Interpreting Revelation*. Grand Rapids: Eerdmans, 1957.

_____. *New Testament Survey*. Revised edition. Edited by Walter M. Dunnett. Grand Rapids: Eerdmans, 1985.

_____, ed. *The Zondervan Pictorial Bible Dictionary*. Grand Rapids: Zondervan, 1963.

_____, ed. *The Zondervan Pictorial Encyclopedia of the Bible*. 5 vols. Grand Rapids: Zondervan, 1975.

Thomas, Robert L. "1, 2 Thessalonians." In *The Expositor's Bible Commentary*. Vol. 11. Edited by Frank E. Gaebelein. Grand Rapids: Zondervan, 1978.

Trattner, Ernest R. *Understanding the Talmud*. Westport, Conn.: Greenwood, 1978.

Unger, Merrill F. *The New Unger's Bible Handbook*. Revised edition. Chicago: Moody Press, 1984.

VanderKam, James C. *The Dead Sea Scrolls Today*. Grand Rapids: Eerdmans, 1994.

Vaughan, Curtis. "Colossians." In *The Expositor's Bible Commentary*. Vol. 11. Edited by Frank E. Gaebelein. Grand Rapids: Zondervan, 1978.

Walton, John H. *Chronological Charts of the Old Testament*. Revised edition. Grand Rapids: Zondervan, 1994.

Watson, George Ronald. *The Roman Soldier*. Ithaca, N.Y.: Cornell University Press, 1969.

Westcott, B. F., and F. Hort. *The New Testament in the Original Greek*. New York: Harper and Brothers, 1881. Reprint, New York: Macmillan, 1922.

Wise, Michael, Martin Abegg Jr., and Edward Cook. *The Dead Sea Scrolls: A New Translation*. San Francisco: HarperSanFrancisco, 1996.

Wood, A. Skevington. "Ephesians." In *The Expositor's Bible Commentary*. Vol. 11. Edited by Frank E. Gaebelein. Grand Rapids: Zondervan, 1978.

Wright, Frederick Adam. *A History of Later Greek Literature from the Death of Alexander in 323 B.C. to the Death of Justinian in 565 A.D.* London: Routledge, 1932.

Subject Index

Name Index

Biblical/Historical

Modern Scholars

We want to hear from you. Please send your comments about this book to us in care of zreview@zondervan.com. Thank you.

ZONDERVAN.com/
AUTHORTRACKER
follow your favorite authors

9 780310 282938